The Original
COPYCAT RECIPES
COOKBOOK

HOW TO MAKE the 200 MOST FAMOUS AND DELICIOUS RESTAURANT DISHES AT HOME. A STEP-BY-STEP COOKBOOK TO PREPARE YOUR FAVORITE POPULAR BRAND-NAMED FOODS AND DRINKS

COPYRIGHT - 2023 - MATT BLACK

This document is geared towards providing exact and reliable information regarding the topic and issue covered. The publication is sold with the idea that the publisher is not required to render accounting, officially permitted, or otherwise, qualified services. If advice is necessary, legal or professional, a practiced individual in the profession should be ordered.

From a Declaration of Principles which was accepted and approved equally by a Committee of the American Bar Association and a Committee of Publishers and Associations.

In no way is it legal to reproduce, duplicate, or transmit any part of this document in either electronic means or printed format. Recording of this publication is strictly prohibited and any storage of this document is not allowed unless with written permission from the publisher. All rights reserved.

The information provided herein is stated to be truthful and consistent, in that any liability, in terms of inattention or otherwise, by any usage or abuse of any policies, processes, or directions contained within is the solitary and utter responsibility of the recipient reader. Under no circumstances will any legal responsibility or blame be held against the publisher for any reparation, damages, or monetary loss due to the information herein, either directly or indirectly.

Respective authors own all copyrights not held by the publisher.

The information herein is offered for informational purposes solely and is universal as so. The presentation of the information is without a contract or any type of guarantee assurance.

The trademarks that are used are without any consent, and the publication of the trademark is without permission or backing by the trademark owner. All trademarks and brands within this book are for clarifying purposes only and are owned by the owners themselves, not affiliated with this document.

APPETIZERS........175

DESSERT........183

SNACK........195

ITALIAN RECIPES........209

MEXICAN RECIPES........217

Let's start!

For A Happy Life...

- 1 🍺 of laughter

- a bag of 🌸

- 1 🥄 of tenderness

- many drops of 💗

<u>Serve daily with generous smiles</u>

Introduction

Copycat recipes have many advantages over original recipes. They are cheaper, they're easier to make, and they taste better. Also, copycat recipes are not copyrighted, and therefore you can share them with others for free.
They are a great way to save money and time when cooking at home. The key is to make sure that you are getting the most bang for your buck when it comes to ingredients. They also allow you not to waste money since you can eat restaurant dishes remaining at home.

Almost all of us are busy, and some, especially moms and students, have very limited time in a day. Using copycat recipes, you can whip up healthy meals for your family in no time with our copycat recipes roundup. All you need is a little inspiration.
Copycat recipes are a great way for you to get creative with your food and be more adventurous in the kitchen. As a matter of fact, they allow you to learn how to cook with ingredients you may not be familiar with. You can get creative and make something unique, or you can follow a recipe and make the dish exactly as it's written. Copycat recipes are also great for people that want to try something new but don't have the time or energy to make something from scratch.
These recipes can also allow you to start your business and make money, for example, through online videos or a website.

The recipes contained in this book are simple, absolutely delicious, and can be made in less than 30 minutes.

Breakfast

IHOP Strawberry & Cream Crepes

Difficulty ●○○

Cost $ $ $

Servings 22 crepes

Preparation Time............ 25 min

Cooking Time................... 60 min

- 1-1/2 cups dairy
- 3 big eggs
- 2 tablespoons butter, thawed
- 1/2 teaspoon lemon extract
- 1-1/4 cups all-purpose flour
- 2 tablespoons sweets
- Dash salt

Topping:
- 1/2 cup sugar
- 2 tablespoon corn starch
- 3/4 cup water
- 1 tbsp. lemon extract

- 1 teaspoon strawberry extract
- 1/4 teaspoon red food coloring, optional
- 4 mugs cut fresh strawberries.

Filling:
- 1 cup heavy whipping cream
- 1 package deal (8 ounces) lotion cheese, relaxed.
- 2 cups confectioners' sugar
- 1 tsp vanilla essence

1. In a large bowl, mix the dairy, eggs, butter and extract. Mix the salt, flour and glucose; add to dairy mixture and blend well. Cover and cool it for 1 hour.
2. Heat up an 8-in, gently oiled. Skillet non-stick over channel heat; pour in 2 tablespoons. Add right into middle of skillet. Turn and lift frying pan to base plate in equal measure.
3. Prepare until top looks dry; turn over and chef longer than 15-20 seconds. Drop onto a rack of coffee. Repeat with the remaining concoction and grease the skillet as required. In between, stack crepes when cold, with polished paper or newspaper towels.
4. In a tiny pan, blend glucose and corn starch; rouse in water and lemon extract until smooth. Offer a boil over tool warm; cook and rouse for 1 minute or until expanded. Add strawberries. In a small bowl, beat the lotion up until stiff optimal develop; reserved.
5. In a sizable bowl, trumped the cream cheese, confectioners' sugar and vanilla up until smooth; crease in beat cream. Spoon 2 rounded tablespoons of loading down the center of each crepe; scroll up. Top with strawberry topping.

Calories 800
Fat 30 g
Carbs 117 g
Protein 19 g

Dunkin Donuts Jelly Doughnuts

Difficulty ● ● ●

Cost $ $ $

Servings 16 pastries

Preparation Time............ 30 min

Cooking Time................... 10 min

- 2 packages (1/4 ounce each) energetic dry yeast
- 1/2 cup cozy water (110 ° to 115 °)
- 1/2 cup warm and comfortable 2% dairy (110 ° to 115 °)
- 1/3 cup butter, softened
- 1-1/3 mugs sweets, split.
- 3 huge egg yolk sacs, room temperature.
- 1 tsp sodium
- 3 to 3-3/4 cups versatile flour
- 3 tablespoons jelly or jam
- 1 large egg white, gently beaten
- Oil for deep-fat frying

1. In a small dish, diffuse in warm and comfortable water. In a large dish, integrate milk, butter, 1/3 cup glucose, egg yolk sacs, salt, yeast mixture and 3 cups of flour; beat up until smooth.
2. Mix in enough staying flour to form a soft dough (do not manipulated).Put in a greased bowl, turning top to grease the moment.
3. Cover and allow progress to be made in a hot place until multiplied, concerning 45 minutes. Blow down on cash. Turn on a surface which is gently floured; knead about 10 times. Dividing cash in half.
4. Roll up to 1/4-in per serving. Density; decreased by 2-1/2- floured in. Cutter rounded. Place 1/2 tsp jelly in the middle of half the cycles; brush sides with colored egg white. Top with remaining circles; force the edges tightly to seal.
5. Place on greased baking slab. Cover and permit climb until multiplied, regarding 45 moments. In an electric skillet or even deep-fat fryer, heat energy oil to 375 °. Fry pastries, a few each time, 1-2 minutes on each side or till gold brownish. Drain towels carefully. Roll hot doughnuts in staying glucose.

Calories 280;
Fat 14g;
Carbs 34g;
Protein 3g

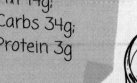

Perkins Restaurant & Bakery Chocolate Silk Pie

Difficulty ● ● ●

Cost $ $ $

Servings 2

Preparation Time............ 25 min

Cooking Time................... 28 min

- 1 (9 inches) pie crust
- 1 jar (7 oz.) marshmallow crème
- 1 cup semisweet chocolate chips
- 1/4 cup butter, cubed
- 2 oz. unsweetened chocolate
- 2 tablespoons strong brewed coffee
- 1 cup heavy whipping cream, whipped

Topping
- 1 cup heavy whipping cream
- 2 tablespoons confectioners' sugar
- Chocolate curls, optional

1. Spread the pie crust in a 9-inches pie plate and cut off the edges extending half-inch beyond the rim of the pie plate; Refrigerate this crust for 30 minutes until all other ingredients are ready;
2. Set the oven's temperature to 425 degrees F for preheating; Cover the crust with a thick foil sheet and add some uncooked rice or dried beans for weight;
3. Bake this crust on the lower rack of the oven for 25 minutes; once baked, remove the foil from the crust and bake again for 3 minutes;
4. Transfer this crust to a wire rack and allow it to cool; Place a heavy saucepan over low heat and add chocolate chips, butter, unsweetened chocolate, coffee, and marshmallow crème;
5. Stir cook until the chocolate is melted and mix well with other ingredients. Remove this mixture from the heat and fold in whipped cream;
6. Mix well and pour this filling into the baked crust. Prepare the topping by beating the cream with confectioner's sugar in a mixing bowl until it forms peaks. Spread the cream topping over the pie and cover it with plastic wrap;
7. Place the pie in the refrigerator for 3 hours. Garnish with chocolate curls and shavings. Slice and serve.

Calories 760;
Fat 66g;
Carbs 54g;
Protein 6g

Delicate croissants

Difficulty ● ● ○

Cost $ $ $

Servings 2

Preparation Time............ 15 min

Cooking Time.................. 10 min

- 1/2 cup sugar
- 1 tablespoon all-purpose flour
- 2 cups heavy whipping cream
- 4 egg yolks, beaten
- 2 scoops vanilla ice cream
- 1 tablespoon vanilla extract
- Berry Sauce

- 2 cups fresh of raspberries
- 2 tablespoons sugar
- French Toast
- 3 eggs
- 4 croissants, split
- 2 tablespoons butter

1. Take a large saucepan and add flour and sugar. Mix them together. Gradually stir in cream and continue mixing until it makes a smooth mixture;
2. Place this pan over medium-high heat and stir cook until it thickens and starts to bubble. Reduce the pan's heat to low and stir cook for 2 minutes, then immediately remove it from the heat;
3. Take another bowl and beat egg yolks in it. Slowly add a small amount of hot cream mixture and mix it well. Return this egg-milk mixture to the saucepan and cook again with occasional stirring until it reaches 160 degrees F.
4. Remove it from the heat then add vanilla and ice cream. Cover this mixture with plastic wrap and allow it to cool. Prepare the berry sauce and add sugar along with raspberries to a saucepan.
5. Cook this mixture on a simmer for 3 minutes; then remove it from the heat. Dip the croissant in the whisked egg mixture and sear them in a griddles pan until golden brown on both the sides;
6. Serve the croissants with a dollop of vanilla cream and berry sauce on top.

Calories 765;
Fat 32g;
Carbs 99g;
Protein 22g

Coco's Bakery Restaurant
Fe Santa Fe Quiche

Difficulty ●● ○

Cost $ $ $

Servings 6

Preparation Time............ 15 min

Cooking Time................... 55 min

- 3 large eggs, beaten
- 1 pastry shell (9 inches), unbaked
- 1/4 teaspoon pepper
- 1 can (2-1/4 ounces) sliced ripe olives, drained
- 1 cup shredded Monterey Jack cheese
- 1-1/2 cups half-and-half cream

- 1 teaspoon salt
- 1 teaspoon chili powder
- 1 tablespoon all-purpose flour
- 1 cup shredded cheddar cheese
- 1 can (4 ounces) chopped green chilies, well drained

1. Sprinkle chili powder over crust's inside. Mix the cheeses with the flour and put them in the crust.
2. Mix the whites, milk, chilies, olives, salt and pepper together. Sprinkle over cheese.
3. Bake for 45-55 minutes at 325 °, or until clean comes out a knife inserted in the middle. Cool for 10 minutes, before the wedges are removed.

Calories 550;
Carbs 40g;
Fat 35g;
Protein 20g

IHOP Stuffed French toast

Difficulty ● ● ○

Cost $ $ $

Servings 6

Preparation Time............ 5 min

Cooking Time................... 25 min

- 1 loaf of French bread
- Splash of milk
- 4 eggs
- 2 tablespoons butter
- Canned strawberry pie filling or fresh strawberries, for garnish

- 1 (24.2-ounce) tub Philadelphia Ready to Eat Cheesecake Filling
- Whipped cream, for garnish

1. Slice bread into slices that are 1" thick. Beat the eggs with milk in a bowl. Dip slices of bread into the egg batter. Attach a few butter pats to a pan, and let it melt.

2. Fry bread on each side for 2-3 minutes, until slightly brown. Put several tablespoons of the cheesecake filling on one piece of the toast. Top on another slice. Garnish with sliced strawberries or top with canned strawberry pie filling. Top with whipped cream.

Calories 850;
Carbs 120g;
Fat 34g;
Protein 15g

Denny Country Fried Steak

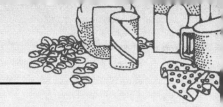

Difficulty ●○○

Cost $ $ $

Servings 4

Preparation Time............ 10 min

Cooking Time.................. 35 min

- 1 pound beef cube steak, dice into 4 pieces
- 1/2 cup buttermilk
- 1 teaspoon salt
- 1 cup flour
- 1/2 teaspoon paprika
- 1/2 teaspoon pepper
- 1/4 cup vegetable oil

1. Make the meat tender by beating it with a mallet or the bottom of a heavy skillet. In a shallow dish, stir the flour, salt, paprika and pepper together. Place the buttermilk in a separate platter.
2. Dredge steaks in the flour mixture, dip in buttermilk and dip in the flour mixture again. Heat up oil over medium-high heat in a large skillet. Cook the steaks on either side for 5 minutes.

Calories 660;
Fat 43g;
Carbs 29g;
Protein 39g

Dunkin Donuts Cinnamon Raisin Bagels

Difficulty ● ● ○

Cost $ $ $

Servings 2

Preparation Time............ 40 min

Cooking Time.................. 30 min

- 1 1/2 cups warm water
- 2 ¾ teaspoons yeast
- 4 cups bread flour
- 1 tablespoon light brown sugar
- 2 teaspoons salt
- 1 teaspoon pure vanilla extract
- ¾ cup raisins
- 3 tablespoons sugar, granulated

- 1 teaspoon ground cinnamon
- 1 tablespoon olive oil
- Water Bath
- 1/2 water
- 1/4 cup honey
- Egg Wash
- 1 egg white
- 1 tablespoon water

1. Take a large-sized mixing bowl and add warm water along with yeast. Mix the yeast mixture and cover it to sit for 5 minutes at room temperature. Place this mixing bowl in the stand mixer under the dough hook. Add vanilla extract, salt, brown sugar and flour and continue beating the mixture for 2 minutes. When all the ingredients come together as a dough, stir in raisins and mix well until dough is smooth and firm. Spread cinnamon and sugar over the working surface and transfer the raisins dough to this surface.
2. Knead the raisins dough for 4 minutes to mix in cinnamon and sugar. Take a glass bowl and grease with cooking spray or oil. Place the raisins and cinnamon dough in the greased bowl and brush the top with cooking oil. Cover the bowl with aluminum foil and leave it at a warm place in the kitchen for 90 minutes.
3. Take two large-sized baking sheets with baking paper; Remove the raised dough from the bowl and knead it well. Divide the kneaded dough into 8 equal-sized pieces and roll each piece into a ball. Spread each ball into a ring with a hole at the center. Place the prepared bagels in the baking sheet and cover them with a kitchen towel .Set the oven's temperature to 425 degrees F for preheating.
4. Prepare a water bath by heating 1/2 water in a cooking pot and cook it to a boil. Add honey and reduce the pot's heat to medium-high heat. Drop 2 bagels at a time into the water bath and cook for 1 minute per side.
5. Remove the cooked bagels from the water bath and place them in the baking sheets. Brush the top of each bagel with egg wash using a pastry brush. Bake all the bagels for 25 minutes in the oven.
6. Remove the crispy baked bagels from the oven and allow them to cool.

Calories 320;
Fat 1g;
Carbs 67g;
Protein 11g

Kneader Chunky Cinnamon French toast

Difficulty ●○○

Cost $ $ $

Servings 8

Preparation Time............ 20 min

Cooking Time.................. 5 min

- 1 bun Kneader's Chunky Cinnamon Bread reduced into 8 cuts (if you do not live near Kneaders, you can only make use of some cinnamon swirl bread)
- 6 large eggs
- 3 cups milk
- 1 tablespoon brownish sweets
- 3/4 teaspoon salt
- 1 Tablespoon vanilla extraction
- 2 Tablespoons butter
- Caramel Syrup
- 1 cup brown sweets
- 1 cup heavy light whipping cream
- 1 cup corn syrup

1. For the French toast: Preheat an electric frying pan to 375 levels F
2. Mix the eggs, butter, brown sugar, salt and vanilla in shallow baking milk.
3. Liquefy butter evenly all over your frying pan. Plunge each slice of bread into a mixture of eggs and completely cover on each side.
4. Place layered bread on a warm frying pan and turn until browned gently on either side. Serve ahead with sugar syrup and whipped cream and sliced strawberries.
5. For the sugar syrup: In a medium pan, blend all syrup ingredients over medium warm. Whip together until smooth and sugar has broken down. Serve hot over French toast.

Calories 415;
Carbs 55g;
Fat 19g;
Protein 12g

Denny Pancake Puppies

Difficulty

Cost $ $ $

Servings 6

Preparation Time........... 10 min

Cooking Time.................. 5 min

- Vegetable oil, for frying
- 1/3 cup milk
- 1 cup Aunt Jemima Original Pancake Mix
- 1 egg
- 1 tablespoon finely chopped white chocolate chips
- 1/2 cup chopped dried blueberries
- Powdered sugar, for dusting

1. In a deep fryer, preheat oil. Combine pancake mixture, milk, and egg into a medium dish. Add the chocolate chips and blueberries and stir. Let the batter sit in to thicken for 10 minutes. Use an oil-coated ice cream scoop to make a batter ball, when the oil is hot, and drop it into the hot oil.
2. Cook for 2 1/2-3 minutes, until the batter is dark brown. Place on paper towels to drain and top with powdered sugar.

Calories 390;
Fat 12;
Carbs 67g;
Protein 6g

California Kitchen Pizza Italian Chopped Salad

Difficulty ●○○

Cost $ $ $

Servings 6

Preparation Time........... 30 min

Cooking Time................... /

- 1 big head (4 cups; 285g) romaine lettuce
- 1 can (15 oz.; 439g) chickpeas (additionally called garbanzo grains), drained pipes and washed
- 1 pint (2 cups; 300g) antique cherry tomatoes cut into quarters
- 1/2 cup (48g) extremely thinly cut reddish onion
- 1 cup (4 oz.; 120g) chopped salami
- 1/2 cup (80g) chopped pork
- 1 cup (5oz, 140g) fresh mozzarella gems, halved
- 1/3 cup (40g) thinly sliced pepperoncini
- 10-12 sizable fresh basil leaves behind

Dressing:
- 2 tablespoons freshly pressed lemon extract
- 2 tablespoons Dijon mustard
- 3 tablespoons cabernet white vinegar
- 3 teaspoons white colored sweets
- 1 tsp dried oregano
- 1 tsp dried out parsley
- 1 clove garlic (1/2 tsp lessened)
- 1/3 cup olive oil
- Sodium and pepper

1. Place every one of the dressing ingredients in a wide-mouth container. Season with salt and pepper— I add 1/2 teaspoon salt, and 1/4 teaspoon pepper. Place the bottle cover, and quickly shake to blend. Sure, place bottle in the refrigerator and outlet there until all set to dress the salad that was tossed.
2. Lettuce:
3. Wash and cut the lettuce. I like to reduce the salad into ribbons (wrap the items right into stogies and afterwards very finely slice) and after that halve the ribbons-- thinner mixed greens parts allow additional surface for the dressing to stick to. Utilize a mixed greens rewriter to ensure the lettuce is 100% dry before including every other ingredient.
4. Tossed Salad Ingredients:
5. Add in the drained pipes and washed chickpeas, quartered cherry tomatoes, very finely cut reddish onion, thinly sliced salami, chopped ham, halved mozzarella gems, and very finely sliced pepperoncini.
6. Chiffonade the basil pieces (find Note 2) and add those right into the tossed salad. Toss the mixed greens and adjust add-ins to personal desire. (The amounts noted are basic tips of how we like this chopped salad. The ideal component of creating this homemade is you can easily add added garnishes to individual preference!).
7. Add Dressing:
8. Cut the dressing from the refrigerator and drink for recombination again. Just apply the dressing to the amount of salad you'll be immediately delighting in. The mixed greens do not fit effectively with dressing so keep it separate until it's ready to eat right away!
9. Surplus Dressing:
10. You may not utilize all the dressing in this tossed salad (outfit to desire). Leftover dressing maintains to a week in the fridge. 1

Calories 313;
Carbs 24g;
Protein 48g;
Fat 82g

Cheddar Honey Butter Croissants

Difficulty ●○○

Cost $ $ $

Servings 12

Preparation Time............ 40 min

Cooking Time.................. 25 min

- 3 1/2 cup all-purpose flour plus more to flour work surface
- 1 1/3 cup milk
- 2 1/4 tsp yeast (1 envelope)
- 1 1/2 tsp salt
- 2 tbsp. vegetable oil
- 1 tbsp. granulated sugar

- 1 1/2 cup butter cold, 3 sticks
- Egg Wash
- 1 egg
- 1 tsp heavy whipping cream
- Honey Butter Drizzle:
- 1/4 cup unsalted butter
- 2 1/2 tbsp. honey
- 3 tbsp. powdered sugar

For The Croissant Dough:

1. Combine flour, milk, yeast, salt, vegetable oil, and sugar using a stand mixer with a dough hook. Mix the dough on low for 3 minutes. If you do not have a stand mixer, mix the ingredients together with a spoon until they begin to thicken, then kneed it with your hands. The dough is ready when it no longer is so sticky that it clings to your fingers or the dough hook. Dough should be tacky, but easy to detach and roll into a ball.

2. Grease a large bowl with butter, and then place the croissant dough ball inside. Cover bowl with plastic wrap and allow dough to rise for 1-2 hours in a warm environment. Tip: I ran my dryer on low heat for 20 minutes, turned it off, and then placed the bowl inside with the door closed.

3. While dough rises, cut each stick of cold butter lengthwise into 3 pieces. Place butter slices in a Ziploc bag (quart sized), arranging them in as close to a flat layer as possible. Using a rolling pin, roll and press the butter so that the edges fuse together and the butter reaches the edges of the bag. This will create a solid 8x8 square of butter. Cut butter out of Ziploc bag, and then wrap the butter square in plastic wrap. Place butter back in the refrigerator until dough is ready.

4. Once dough has risen, the next step is to "laminate" the dough, which is a special technique of folding the cold butter within the croissant dough. Once dough has been laminated, refrigerate it overnight. Remove cold dough from refrigerator. Prepare 2 baking sheets by lining them with parchment paper. Dough must remain cold while working (to prevent butter within from melting), so before beginning, divide the dough in half. Keep one half to work with and place the other half in the refrigerator so that it remains cold until ready to be used.

5. Generously flour your work space. Place dough down and roll into a 7 x 20" rectangle, using more flour to prevent sticking as necessary. Cut triangles within the dough, making the small point about 1/4 inch wide and the wide end about 4-5 inches wide. Once cut, roll croissants starting from the wide base toward the small point. Place croissants on the baking sheet 2 inches apart. If desired, curl the ends of the croissant for a more decorative look. Remove the other half of the dough from the refrigerator and repeat the same steps.

6. Prepare egg wash by whisking together egg and cream. Coat croissants generously with egg wash using a pastry brush.

7. Allow croissants to rise for another 1-3 hours at room temperature. Dough will puff slightly and should wiggle if baking dish is lightly shaken. Preheat oven to 375 F. Bake croissants for 25-35 minutes or until tops are golden brown.

8. or The Honey Butter Drizzle:

9. In a microwave safe bowl, heat butter until melted, about 45 seconds. Whisk in honey and powdered sugar. If the honey will not fully dissolve, heat the sauce for another 20 seconds.

10. Putting It All Together:

11. Serve croissants warm with honey butter drizzled on top or as a dipping sauce on the side.

Panera Bread Caramel Pecan Rolls

Difficulty ● ● ○

Cost $ $ $

Servings 2-4

Preparation Time............ 15 min

Cooking Time.................. 25 min

- 1 cup of milk
- 1/4 cup water
- 1/4 cup sugar
- 1/4 cup butter
- 1/6 cup cornmeal
- 1 teaspoon salt
- 3 1/2 cups all-purpose flour
- 1 package (1/4 oz.) active dry yeast

- 1 large egg
- **Topping**
- 1 cup packed brown sugar
- 1/4 cup butter
- 1/4 cup milk
- 1/2 cup pecans, chopped
- **Filling**
- 1/8 cup butter, softened
- 1/4 cup sugar
- 1 teaspoon ground cinnamon

1. Take a suitable-sized saucepan and place it over medium-high heat. Add milk, water, sugar, butter, cornmeal, and salt to the saucepan. Stir cook this cornmeal mixture to a boil, then remove it from the heat and allow it to cool. Meanwhile, mix 2 cups flour with yeast in a mixing bowl;

2. Beat the cornmeal mixture in a mixing bowl on low speed until smooth. Add flour mixture to the cornmeal and mix well until smooth. Stir in 1 cup flour, and eggs then whisk well until it makes soft dough. Transfer this cornmeal dough to a lightly floured surface and knead it for 8 minutes;

3. Grease glass bowl with cooking oil and place the dough in the bowl. Cover the cornmeal dough with a plastic sheet and leave it for 1 hour at a warm place in the kitchen. Meanwhile, prepare the topping by mixing sugar, butter, and milk in a small bowl. Pour this topping into a greased 8 inches baking pan and drizzle pecans on top;

4. Remove the flour dough from the bowl and divide it into two halves. Roll each dough piece into 8X5 inches rectangle. Top each rectangle with butter and then drizzle cinnamon and sugar over this layer. Now roll each dough sheet from its long side and pinch the seams to seal. Slice each roll into 4 slices to get a shape of a pinwheel. Place these cinnamon rolls in the prepared pan, layered with topping mixture;

5. Cover the cinnamon rolls with a kitchen towel and leave them for 30 minutes. Now bake the cinnamon rolls for 25 minutes in the oven at 375 degrees F. Once baked, remove the cinnamon rolls pan from the oven and leave it for 1 minute. Flip the pan over a plate and remove it from the top. Serve.

Calories 720,
Carbs 69g,
Fat 46g;
Protein 11g

IHOP Original Buttermilk Pancake

Difficulty ● ○ ○

Cost $ $ $

Servings 8

Preparation Time........... 10 min

Cooking Time.................. 10 min

- 1 1/4 cups sifted all-purpose flour
- 1 teaspoon baking powder
- 1 teaspoon baking soda
- 1 large egg, beaten
- 1 1/4 cups buttermilk
- 1/8 Teaspoon salt
- 3 Tablespoons sugar
- 2 Tablespoons butter, melted

1. Firstly, put the flour, baking powder, baking soda and salt together in a big pot. Combine egg and buttermilk in a medium saucepan. Whisk in before mixing. Add mixture to the rice, stirring until smooth. Add the melted butter and sugar to whisk and bake until mixed.

2. Place on medium-low heat a griddle or non-stick skillet—grease griddle with spray or butter to cook. Drop one-fourth cup batter into the pan and spread into a circle of 5 inches. Cook until surface bubbles begin to form, and edges start to brown. Flip softly to the other hand and switch to brown. Repeat with batter left over. Serve with simmering butter and sweet syrup.

Nutrition:
Calories 670;
Fat 24g;
Carbs 94g;
Protein 4g

IHOP Crepes

Difficulty ●○○

Cost $ $ $

Servings 4

Preparation Time............ 10 min

Cooking Time.................. 20 min

- **1 cup all-purpose flour**
- **2 eggs**
- **1/2 cup milk**
- **1/4 teaspoon salt**
- **1/2 cup water**
- **2 tablespoon melted butter**

1. Mix the flour and eggs in a bowl until combined. Add milk and water and then mix again until evenly combined. Finally, finish off the batter with butter and salt applied. Keep whisking until the batter gets smooth.

2. Heat a non-stick saucepan and add the butter. When the butter has heated a little, ladle some of the batter over it. Spread the batter slightly by tilting the pan, and cook the bottom side until golden brown. Now turn the crepe onto the other side to get the same color. Make this way all the crepes, and serve soft.

Calories 1120;
Fat 75g;
Carbs 52g;
Protein 60g

IHOP's Buttermilk Pancake

Difficulty ● ○ ○

Cost $ $ $

Servings 8 to 10

Preparation Time............ 5 min

Cooking Time................... 8 min

- 1 1/4 cups all-purpose flour
- 1 teaspoon baking soda
- 1 teaspoon baking powder
- 1 1/4 cups granulated sugar
- 1 pinch salt

- 1 egg
- 1 1/4 cups buttermilk
- 1/4 cup cooking oil

1. Preheat your pan by leaving it over medium heat while you are preparing the pancake batter. Incorporate all the dry ingredients together, then combine all of your wet ingredients together as well.

2. Carefully combine the dry mixture into the wet mixture until everything is mixed together completely. Melt some butter in your pan.

3. Slowly pour batter into the pan until you have a 5-inch circle. Flip the pancake when its edges seem to have hardened. Cook the other side of the hotcake as well. Repeat steps six through eight until your batter is finished. Serve with softened butter and maple syrup.

180 Calories
7.9g Fat
23.2g Carbs
4.1g Protein

Starbucks's Marble Pound Cake

Difficulty ● ● ●

Cost $ $ $

Servings 16

Preparation Time............ 10 min

Cooking Time.................. 30 min

- 4 1/2 cups cake flour
- 2 teaspoons baking powder
- 1/8 Teaspoon salt
- 6 ounces semisweet chocolate, finely chopped

- 2 cups unsalted butter, softened
- 3 cups granulated sugar
- 1 tablespoon vanilla
- 1 lemon, grated for zest
- 10 large eggs
- 2 tablespoons orange liquor OR milk

1. Assemble your ingredients, and then: Preheat the oven to 350F; Grease a 10×4-inch tube pan;
2. Line the pan's bottom with greased wax paper, and Flour the entire pan. Sift together the cake flour, baking powder, and salt in a medium-sized bowl—this is your dry mixture.
3. Melt the chocolate in a medium-sized bowl, then beat in the butter. When it is smooth, mix in the sugar, lemon zest, and vanilla until the liquid mixture is uniform.
4. Beat eggs two at a time, until the mixture looks curdled.
5. Pour half of your dry mixture into your liquid mixture and mix until blended.
6. Add the orange liquor and the rest of the dry mixture. Continue beating the mixture.
7. When the mixture is blended, use a spatula to start folding it—this is your batter.
8. Set aside 4 cups of the batter. Whisk the softened chocolate with the batter.
9. Now that you have a light batter and a dark batter, place the batter into the tube pan by the spoonful, alternating between the two colors.
10. When the pan is full, shake it slightly to level the batter. Run a knife through the batter to marble it.
11. Put the dish within the stove and heat for an hour and 15 minutes. In case there are still a few damp pieces on the toothpick after you take it out, at that point, the cake is ready.
12. Remove the cake and leave it to rest overnight.

582 Calories
32g Fat
69g Carbs
8.6g Protein

IHOP's Scrambled Egg

Difficulty ●○○

Cost $ $ $

Servings 1

Preparation Time............ 5 min

Cooking Time................... 5 min

- 1/4 cup pancake mix
- 1-2 tablespoons butter
- 6 large eggs
- Salt and pepper, to taste

1. Thoroughly beat the pancake mix and the eggs together until no lumps or clumps remain.
2. Butter a pan over medium heat. Add in the egg mixture in the middle of the pan. Add the salt and pepper and let the mixture sit for about a minute.
3. When the egg starts cooking, start pushing the edges of the mixture toward the middle of the pan. Continue until the entire mixture is cooked. Serve and enjoy.

870 Calories
54g Total Fat
9g Carbohydrates
69g Protein

Starbucks's Chocolate Cinnamon Bread

Difficulty ●●○

Cost $ $ $

Servings 16

Preparation Time............ 15 min

Cooking Time.................. 60 min

Bread:
- 1/2 cups unsalted butter
- 3 cups granulated sugar
- 5 large eggs
- 2 cups flour
- 1 1/4 cups processed cocoa
- 1 tablespoon ground cinnamon
- 1 teaspoon salt
- 1/2 teaspoon baking powder
- 1/2 teaspoon baking soda
- 1/4 cup water
- 1 cup buttermilk
- 1 teaspoon vanilla extract

Topping:
- 1/4 cup granulated sugar
- 1/2 teaspoon cinnamon
- 1/2 teaspoon processed cocoa
- 1/8 Teaspoon ginger, ground
- 1/8 Teaspoon cloves, ground

1. Grease and preheat the oven to 350 degrees and line the bottoms of the pans with wax paper.
2. Cream the sugar by beating it with the butter. Beat the eggs into the mixture one at a time. Sift the flour, cocoa, cinnamon, salt, baking powder, and baking soda into a large bowl.
3. In another bowl, whisk together the water, buttermilk, and vanilla. Make a well in the dry mixture and start pouring in the wet mixtures a little at a time, while whisking.
4. When the mixture starts becoming doughy, divide it in two, and transfer it to the pans.
5. Combine together all the topping and sprinkle evenly on top of the mixture in both pans.
6. Bake until the bread has set.

370 Calories
14g Fat
59g Carbs
7g Protein

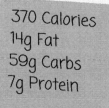

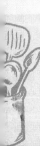

Waffle House's Waffle

Difficulty ● ● ●

Cost $ $ $

Servings 6

Preparation Time............ 15 min

Cooking Time.................. 60 min

- 1 1/2 cups all-purpose flour
- 1 teaspoon salt
- 1/2 teaspoon baking soda
- 1 egg
- 1/2 cup + 1 tablespoon granulated white sugar
- 2 tablespoons butter, softened

- 2 tablespoons shortening
- 1/2 cup half-and-half
- 1/2 cup milk
- 1/4 cup buttermilk
- 1/4 teaspoon vanilla
-

1. Prepare the dry mixture by sifting the flour into a bowl and mixing it with the salt and baking soda.
2. Lightly beat an egg until it becomes frothy, beat in the butter, sugar, and shortening. When the mixture is thoroughly mixed, beat in the half-and-half, vanilla, milk, and buttermilk. Continue beating the mixture until it is smooth.
3. While beating the wet mixture, slowly pour in the dry mixture, making sure to mix thoroughly and remove all the lumps.
4. Chill the batter overnight (optional but recommended; if you can't chill the mixture overnight, leave it for at least 15 to 20 minutes).
5. Take the batter out of the refrigerator. Preheat and grease your waffle iron.
6. Cook each waffle for three to four minutes. Serve with butter and syrup.

313 Calories
12g Total Fat
45g Carbs
5.9g Protein

Mimi's Café Santa Fé Omelet

Difficulty ● ● ○

Cost $ $ $

Servings 1

Preparation Time............ 10 min

Cooking Time.................. 10 min

- Chipotle Sauce:
- 1 cup marinara or tomato sauce
- ¾ cup water
- 1/2 cup chipotle in adobo sauce
- 1 teaspoon kosher salt
- Omelet:
- 1 tablespoon onions, diced
- 1 tablespoon jalapeños, diced
- 2 tablespoons cilantro, chopped
- 2 tablespoons tomatoes, diced

- 1/4 cup fried corn tortillas, cut into strips
- 3 eggs, beaten
- 2 slices cheese
- 1 dash of salt and pepper
- Garnish:
- 2 ounces chipotle sauce, hot
- 1/4 cup fried corn tortillas, cut into strips
- 1 tablespoon sliced green onions
- 1 tablespoon guacamole

1. Cook butter over medium heat, making sure to coat the entire pan. Sauté the jalapeños, cilantro, tomatoes, onions, and tortilla strips for about a minute.
2. Pour the eggs, seasoning them with salt and pepper and stirring occasionally. Flip the omelet when it has set. Place the cheese on the top half.
3. When the cheese starts to become melty, fold the omelet in half and transfer to a plate. Garnish the omelet with chipotle sauce, guacamole, green onions, and corn tortillas.

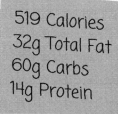

519 Calories
32g Total Fat
60g Carbs
14g Protein

Alice Springs Chicken from Outback

Difficulty ● ○ ○

Cost $ $ $

Servings 4

Preparation Time............ 10 min

Cooking Time.................... 10 min

Sauce:
- 1/2 cup Dijon mustard
- 1/2 cup honey
- 1/4 cup mayonnaise
- 1 teaspoon fresh lemon juice

Chicken preparation:
- 4 chicken breast, boneless and skinless
- 2 tablespoons butter

- 1 tablespoon olive oil
- 8 ounces fresh mushrooms, sliced
- 4 slices bacon, cooked and cut into 2-inch pieces
- 2 1/2 cups Monterrey Jack cheese, shredded
- Parsley for serving (optional)

1. Preheat oven to 400 °F. Mix together ingredients for the sauce in a bowl.
2. Put the chicken in a Ziploc bag, then add the sauce into the bag until only 1/4 cup is left. Keep the remaining sauce in a container, cover, and refrigerate. Make sure to seal the Ziploc bag tightly and shake gently until chicken is coated with sauce. Let it chill for 2 hours.
3. Cook butter in a pan over medium heat. Toss in mushrooms and cook for 5 minutes or until brown. Set aside, then transfer on a plate.
4. In an oven-safe pan, heat oil. Place marinated chicken flat in the pan and cook for 5 minutes on each side or until both sides turn golden brown.
5. Top with even amounts of mushroom, bacon, and cheese. Cover pan with oven-safe lid, then bake for 10 to 15 minutes until chicken is cooked through. Remove lid and bake an additional 1-3 minutes until the cheese is all melted.
6. Transfer onto a plate. Serve with remaining sauce on the side. Sprinkle chicken with parsley if desired

888 Calories
56g Total Fat
41g Carbs
59g Protein

IHOP's Healthy
"Harvest Grain 'N Nut" Pancakes

Difficulty ●●○

Cost $ $ $

Servings 4

Preparation Time............ 5 min

Cooking Time.................. 5 min

- 1 teaspoon olive oil
- ¾ cup oats, powdered
- ¾ cup whole wheat flour
- 2 teaspoons baking soda
- 1 teaspoon baking powder
- 1/2 teaspoon salt
- 1 1/2 cup buttermilk

- 1/4 cup vegetable oil
- 1 egg
- 1/4 cup sugar
- 3 tablespoons almonds, finely sliced
- 3 tablespoons walnuts, sliced
- Syrup for serving

1. Heat oil in a pan over medium heat. While the pan preheats, pulverize oats in a blender until powdered. Then, add to a large bowl with flour, baking soda, baking powder, and salt. Mix well.
2. Add buttermilk, oil, egg, and sugar in a separate bowl. Mix with an electric mixer until creamy. Mix in wet ingredients with dry ingredients, then add nuts. Mix everything together with the electric mixer.
3. Scoop 1/3 cup of batter and cook in the hot pan for at least 2 minutes or until both sides turn golden brown. Transfer onto a plate, then repeat for the remaining batter. Serve with syrup.

433 Calories
24g Total Fat
46g Carbs
12g Protein

McDonald's Sausage Egg McMuffin

Difficulty ●○○

Cost $ $ $

Servings 4

Preparation Time............ 10 min

Cooking Time................... 15 min

- 4 English muffins, cut in half horizontally
- 4 slices American processed cheese
- 1/2 tablespoon oil
- 1-pound ground pork, minced
- 1/2 teaspoon dried sage, ground
- 1/2 teaspoon dried thyme
- 1 teaspoon onion powder
- ¾ teaspoon black pepper
- ¾ teaspoon salt
- 1/2 teaspoon white sugar
- 4 large 1/3-inch onion ring slices
- 4 large eggs
- 2 tablespoons water

1. Preheat oven to 300°F. Cover one half of the muffin with cheese, leaving one half uncovered. Transfer both halves to a baking tray. Place in oven.

2. For the sausage patties, use your hands to mix pork, sage, thyme, onion powder, pepper, salt, and sugar in a bowl. Form into 4 patties. Make sure they are slightly larger than the muffins.

3. Heat oil in a pan. Cook patties on both sides for at least 2 minutes each or until all sides turn brown. Remove the muffin tray from the oven. Place cooked sausage patties on top of the cheese on muffins. Return tray to the oven.

4. In the same pan, position onion rings flat into a single layer. Crack one egg inside each of the onion rings to make them round. Add water carefully into the sides of the pan and cover. Cook for 2 minutes.

5. Remove the muffin tray from the oven. Add eggs on top of patties, then top with the other muffin half. Serve warm.

453 Calories
15g Total Fat
67g Carbs
15g Protein

Starbucks' Spinach and Feta Breakfast Wraps

Difficulty ● ● ●

Cost $ $ $

Servings 6

Preparation Time............ 5 min

Cooking Time.................... 20 min

- 10 ounces spinach leaves
- 1 14 1/2-ounce can dice tomatoes, drained
- 3 tablespoons cream cheese
- 10 egg whites
- 1/2 teaspoon oregano
- 1/2 teaspoon garlic salt
- 1/8 teaspoon pepper
- 6 whole wheat tortillas
- 4 tablespoons feta cheese, crumbled
- Cooking Spray

1. Apply a light coating of cooking spray to a pan. Cook spinach leaves on medium-high heat for 5 minutes or until leaves wilt, then stir in tomatoes and cream cheese. Cook for an additional 5 minutes or until cheese is melted completely. Remove from pan and place into a glass bowl and cover. Set aside.

2. In the same pan, add egg whites, oregano, salt, and pepper. Stir well and cook at least 5 minutes or until eggs are scrambled. Remove from heat.

3. Microwave tortillas for 30 seconds or until warm. Place egg whites, spinach and tomato mixture, and feta in the middle of the tortillas. Fold sides inwards, like a burrito. Serve.

157 Calories
3g Total Fat
19g Carbs
14g Protein

Jimmy Dean's
Homemade Pork Sage Sausage

Difficulty ● ● ○

Cost $ $ $

Servings 4

Preparation Time............ 5 min

Cooking Time................... 20 min

- **1-pound ground pork**
- **1 teaspoon salt**
- **1/2 teaspoon dried parsley**
- **1/4 teaspoon rubbed sage**
- **1/4 teaspoon black pepper, ground**
- **1/4 teaspoon dried thyme**
- **1/4 teaspoon coriander**
- **1/4 teaspoon seasoned salt**

1. **Mix all ingredients in a bowl. Shape into patties. Then, cook in a pan on medium heat until meat is brown on both sides and cooked through. Serve.**

313 Calories
24g Total Fat
4g Carbs
19g Protein

Panera Power Breakfast Sandwich

Difficulty ●○○

Cost $

Servings 1

Preparation Time........... 5 min

Cooking Time................... 20 min

- 2 egg whites
- 1 teaspoon butter, divided in half
- 1 bagel thin, cut in half
- Mustard
- 1/4 avocado, sliced
- 1 large tomato slice
- 4 spinach leaves
- 1 slice Swiss cheese

1. Cook egg whites for about 1 minute in a small tightly covered custard cup in the microwave. Apply 1/2 teaspoon butter to both thin halves of the bagel. Coat inside of top bagel half with mustard and the other with avocado. Place egg whites, tomato, spinach leaves, and cheese on the bottom bagel thin. Top with another thin half of bagel.

2. Coat a heated pan with a thin layer of cooking spray, pan fry sandwich on medium-high heat for 3 minutes on each side or until golden brown and cheese is melted. I use a Panini press for this step. Serve immediately.

277 Calories
10g Total Fat
30g Carbs
22g Protein

McDonald's McGriddle Breakfast Sandwich

Difficulty ● ○ ○

Cost $ $ $

Servings 4

Preparation Time............ 60 min

Cooking Time................... 15 min

- 1/2 cup maple syrup
- 1 cup flour
- 1 teaspoon baking powder
- 1/2 teaspoon baking soda
- 1 cup buttermilk
- 2 tablespoons butter, melted

- 1 egg
- Softened butter to grease the mold
- 4 slices American cheese
- 4 eggs, scrambled
- 4 strips bacon, cooked and cut in half

1. Line a baking tray with parchment paper and set aside.
2. Add maple syrup to a pot and bring to a boil over medium heat while stirring often. Keep stirring the syrup even when already boiling. At about 230 ºF, after about a minute of boiling, the syrup will appear a bit darker, and the boiling will lessen to some degree. Cook for about 2 more minutes or until the syrup becomes darker and begins to smell a bit like caramel. It is ready to be removed from heat once it reaches 265 ºF.
3. Pour maple syrup onto the prepared baking sheet. Spread evenly in a thin layer with a spatula. Refrigerate until cool. Flip the syrup over, with parchment paper now on top. Then peel off the paper and break the solidified syrup into tiny pieces.
4. To make the pancakes, combine flour, baking powder, and baking soda in a large bowl. Set aside.
5. In another bowl, add buttermilk, butter, and egg. Mix together until fully combined. Then pour onto dry ingredients and mix well until incorporated.
6. Preheat electric griddle to medium-high heat.
7. Coat insides of round molds with softened butter, then place on a hot griddle coated with butter over medium heat. Add about 2 tablespoons pancake batter into each mold, then sprinkle maple crystals on top. Afterward, add 2 more tablespoons of pancake batter on top, sandwiching the maple crystals inside the pancakes.
8. Once bubbles form and edges look cooked, remove molds and flip pancakes. Cook for an additional 1 to 2 minutes.
9. To assemble the sandwiches, add cheese, scrambles egg, and bacon on pancake, then top with another pancake. Serve immediately.

Daddy's Blueberry Buttermilk Pancakes

Difficulty ●○○

Cost $ $ $

Servings 12

Preparation Time............ 15 min

Cooking Time.................. 10 min

- 1 cup all-purpose flour.
- 3 tbsps. Cornmeal.
- 3 tablespoons quick-cooking oats.
- 3 tbsps. Sugar.
- 1 teaspoon baking powder.
- 1/2 tsp cooking soda.
- 1/2 tsp sodium.

- Dash ground nutmeg.
- 1 sizable egg.
- 1-1/2 cups buttermilk.
- 2 tbsps. Canola oil.
- 1 teaspoon vanilla remove.
- 1 cup new or even frosted blueberries.

1. In a big bowl, whip the 1st 8 ingredients. In one more dish, whip egg, buttermilk, oil, and vanilla up until blended.
2. Add to flour mixture; stir only till moistened (batter is going to be lumpy). Permit cool for 15 mins.
3. Lightly grease a frying pan or huge nonstick skillet; heat over tool heat.
4. Rouse blueberries batter right in. Put the batter on griddle or frying pan by 1/4 cups. Cook before blisters start to blister ahead.
5. The bottoms stick out and become brown gold. Switch; cook brown until edge

332 calories
10g fat
52g carbs
18g sugars

Aunt Betty's Blueberry Muffins

Difficulty ● ● ●

Cost $ $ $

Servings 12

Preparation Time............ 15 min

Cooking Time................... 20 min

- 1/2 cup out-of-date oatmeal.
- 1/2 cup orange extract.
- 1 huge egg, room temperature.
- 1/2 cup canola oil.
- 1/2 cup sugar.
- 1-1/2 mugs all-purpose flour.
- 1-1/4 teaspoons cooking powder.
- 1/2 teaspoon salt.

- 1/4 teaspoon cooking soda.
- 1 cup clean or frosted blueberries.
- Topping:
- 2 tablespoons sugar.
- 1/2 teaspoon ground cinnamon.

1. Combine the oats and orange juice in a wide bowl; let stand 5 Moments. Beat in the egg, olive oil, and sugar until mixed. Merge the Cover with flour, baking powder, salt, and baking soda; add oat mixture

2. Just until they're moist. Blueberries fold in. Fill two-thirds full of muffin cups wrapped in greased or parchment. Merge the topping ingredient; brush over the batter. Bake at 20-25 ° C minutes or until a toothpick is inserted in the middle.

3. Remove from pan to wire rack for 5 minutes before cooling. Serve warm.

208 calories,
10g fat
18mg cholesterol
28g carbs

Pasta

Pesto Cavatappi
from Noodles & Company

Difficulty ● ○ ○

Cost $ $ $

Servings 8

Preparation Time............ 5 min

Cooking Time................... 20 min

- 4 quarts water
- 1 tablespoon salt
- 1 pound macaroni pasta
- 1 teaspoon olive oil
- 1 large tomato, finely chopped
- 4 ounce mushrooms, finely chopped

- 1/4 cup chicken broth
- 1/4 cup dry white wine
- 1/4 cup heavy cream
- 1 cup pesto
- 1 cup Parmesan cheese, grated

1. Add water and salt to a pot. Bring to a boil. Put in pasta and cook for 10 minutes or until al dente. Drain and set aside.
2. In a pan, heat oil. Sauté tomatoes and mushrooms for 5 minutes. Pour in broth, wine, and cream. Bring to a boil. Reduce heat to medium and simmer for 2 minutes or until mixture is thick. Stir in pesto and cook for another 2 minutes. Toss in pasta. Mix until fully coated.
3. Transfer onto plates and sprinkle with Parmesan cheese.

Calories 637,
Total Fat 42 g,
Carbs 48 g,
Protein 19 g,
Sodium 1730 mg

Cajun Chicken Pasta from Chili's

Difficulty ● ● ○

Cost $ $ $

Servings 4

Preparation Time............ 10 min

Cooking Time.................... 20 min

- 2 chicken breasts, boneless and skinless
- 1 tablespoon olive oil, divided
- 1 tablespoon Cajun seasoning
- 3 quarts water
- 1/2 tablespoon salt
- 8 ounces penne pasta
- 2 tablespoons unsalted butter
- 3 garlic cloves, minced
- 1 cup heavy cream

- 1/2 teaspoon lemon zest
- 1/4 cup Parmesan cheese, shredded
- Salt and black pepper, to taste
- 1 tablespoon oil
- 2 Roma tomatoes, diced
- 2 tablespoons parsley chopped

1. Place chicken in a Ziploc bag. Add 1 tablespoon oil and Cajun seasoning. Using your hands, combine chicken and mixture until well-coated. Seal tightly and set aside to marinate.
2. Cook pasta in a pot filled with salt and boiling water. Follow package instructions. Drain and set aside.
3. In a skillet, heat butter over medium heat. Sauté garlic for 1 minute or until aromatic. Slowly add cream, followed by lemon zest. Cook for 1 minute, stirring continuously until fully blended. Toss in Parmesan cheese. Mix until sauce is a little thick, then add salt and pepper. Add pasta and combine until well-coated. Transfer onto a bowl and keep warm.
4. In a separate skillet, heat remaining oil. Cook chicken over medium-high heat for about 5 minutes on each side or until fully cooked through. Transfer onto chopping board and cut into thin strips.
5. Top pasta with chicken and sprinkle with tomatoes and parsley on top.
6. Serve.

Calories 655,
Total Fat 38 g,
Carbs 47 g,
Protein 31 g,
Sodium 359 mg

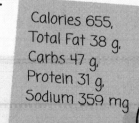

Chow Mein from Panda Express

Difficulty ● ○ ○

Cost $ $ $

Servings 4

Preparation Time........... 10 min

Cooking Time.................. 10 min

- 8 quarts water
- 12 ounces Yakisoba noodles
- 1/4 cup soy sauce
- 3 garlic cloves, finely chopped
- 1 tablespoon brown sugar
- 2 teaspoons ginger, grated

- 1/4 teaspoon white pepper, ground
- 2 tablespoons olive oil
- 1 onion, finely chopped
- 3 celery stalks, sliced on the bias
- 2 cups cabbage, chopped

1. In a pot, bring water to a boil. Cook Yakisoba noodles for about 1 minute until noodles separate. Drain and set aside.
2. Combine soy sauce, garlic, brown sugar, ginger, and white pepper in a bowl.
3. In a pan, heat oil on medium-high heat. Sauté onion and celery for 3 minutes or until soft. Add cabbage and stir-fry for an additional minute. Mix in noodles and soy sauce mixture. Cook for 2 minutes, stirring continuously until noodles are well-coated.
4. Transfer into bowls. Serve.

Calories 382,
Total Fat 8 g,
Carbs 72 g,
Protein 14 g,
Sodium 1194 mg

Rattlesnake Pasta from Pizzeria Uno

Difficulty ● ● ●

Cost $ $ $

Servings 6

Preparation Time............ 5 min

Cooking Time.................. 25 min

Pasta:
- 4 quarts
- 1 pound penne pasta
- 1 dash of salt

Chicken:
- 2 tablespoons butter
- 2 cloves garlic, finely chopped
- 1/2 tablespoon Italian seasoning
- 1 pound chicken breast, boneless and skinless, cut into small squares

Sauce:
- 4 tablespoons butter
- 2 cloves garlic, finely chopped
- 1/4 cup all-purpose flour
- 1 tablespoon salt
- ¾ teaspoon white pepper
- 2 cups milk
- 1 cup half-and-half
- ¾ cup Parmesan cheese, shredded
- 8 ounces Colby cheese, shredded
- 3 jalapeno peppers, chopped

1. In a pot of boiling water, add salt, and cook pasta according to package instructions. Drain well and set aside.

2. To prepare the chicken, heat butter in a pan. Sauté garlic and Italian seasoning for 1 minute. Add chicken and cook 5-7 minutes or until cooked thoroughly, flipping half way through. Transfer onto a plate once. Set aside.

3. In the same pan, prepare the sauce. Add butter and heat until melted. Stir in garlic and cook for 30 seconds. Then, add flour, salt, and pepper. Cook for 2 more minutes, stirring continuously. Pour in milk and half-and-half. Keep stirring until sauce turns thick and smooth.

4. Toss in chicken, jalapeno peppers, and pasta. Stir until combined.

Calories 835,
Total Fat 44 g,
Carbs 72 g,
Protein 40 g,
Sodium 1791 mg

Copycat Kung Pao Spaghetti from California Pizza Kitchen

Difficulty ● ○ ○

Cost $ $ $

Servings 4

Preparation Time............ 10 min

Cooking Time.................. 20 min

- 1 pound spaghetti
- 2 tablespoons vegetable oil
- 3 chicken breasts, boneless and skinless
- Salt and pepper, to taste
- 4 garlic cloves, finely chopped
- 1/2 cup dry roasted peanuts
- 6 green onions, cut into half-inch pieces
- 10-12 Dried bird eyes hot peppers

Sauce:
1/2 cup soy sauce
- 1/2 cup chicken broth
- 1/2 cup dry sherry
- 2 tablespoons red chili paste with garlic
- 1/4 cup sugar
- 2 tablespoons red wine vinegar
- 2 tablespoons cornstarch
- 1 tablespoon sesame oil

1. Follow instructions on package to cook spaghetti noodles. Drain and set aside.
2. Add oil to a large pan over medium-high heat. Generously season chicken with salt and pepper, then add to pan once hot. Cook for about 3 to 4 minutes. Turn chicken over and cook for another 3 to 4 minutes. Remove from heat and allow to cool.
3. Mix together all sauce ingredients in a bowl.
4. Once chicken is cool enough to handle, chop chicken into small pieces. Set aside.
5. Return pan to heat. Add garlic and sauté for about 1 minute until aromatic. Pour in prepared sauce, then stir. Once boiling, lower heat and allow to simmer for about 1 to 2 minutes or until liquid thickens. Add pasta, cooked chicken, peanuts, hot peppers, and scallions. Mix well.
6. Serve.

Calories 548,
Total fat 22 g,
Carbs 67 g,
Protein 15 g,

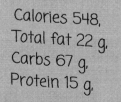

Three Cheese Chicken Penne from Applebee's

Difficulty ●○○

Cost $ $ $

Servings 4

Preparation Time............ 10 min

Cooking Time.................. 20 min

- 2 boneless skinless chicken breasts
- 1 cup Italian salad dressing
- 3 cups penne pasta
- 6 tablespoons olive oil, divided
- 15 ounces Alfredo sauce

- 8 ounces combination mozzarella, Parmesan, and provolone cheeses, grated
- 4 roma tomatoes, seeded and diced
- 4 tablespoons fresh basil, diced
- 2 cloves garlic, finely chopped
- Shredded parmesan cheese for serving

This Alfredo-style penne pasta is oozing with three different Italian cheeses, topped with tomatoes and basil, making it a sure-fire favorite among family dinners.

1. Preheat oven to 350°F.
2. In a bowl, add chicken then drizzle with Italian dressing. Mix to coat chicken with dressing fully. Cover using plastic wrap and keep inside refrigerator overnight but, if you're in a hurry, at least 2 hours is fine.
3. Follow instructions on package to cook penne pasta. Drain, then set aside.
4. Brush 3 tablespoons oil onto grates of grill then preheat to medium-high heat. Add marinated chicken onto grill, discarding the marinade. Cook chicken until both sides are fully cooked and internal temperature measures 165°F. Remove from grill. Set aside until cool enough to handle. Then, cut chicken into thin slices.
5. In a large bowl, add cooked noodles, Alfredo sauce, and grilled chicken. Mix until combined.
6. Drizzle remaining oil onto large casserole pan, then pour noodle mixture inside. Sprinkle cheeses on top. Bake for about 15-20 minutes or until cheese turns a golden and edges of mixture begins to bubble. Remove from oven.
7. Mix tomatoes, basil, and garlic in a bowl. Add on top of pasta.
8. Sprinkle parmesan cheese before serving.

Calories 1402,
Total fat 93 g,
Carbs 91 g,
Protein 62 g,

Boston Market Mac n' Cheese

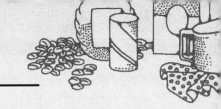

Difficulty ●●●

Cost $ $ $

Servings 6

Preparation Time............ 10 min

Cooking Time................... 20 min

- 1 8-ounce package spiral pasta
- 2 tablespoons butter
- 2 tablespoons all-purpose flour
- 1 ¾ cups whole milk
- 1 1/4 cups diced processed cheese like Velveeta™
- 1/4 teaspoon dry mustard
- 1/2 teaspoon onion powder
- 1 teaspoon salt
- Pepper, to taste

1. Cook pasta according to package instructions. Drain, then set aside.
2. To prepare sauce make the roux with four and butter over medium-low heat in a large deep skillet. Add milk and whisk until well blended. Add cheese, mustard, salt, and pepper. Keep stirring until smooth.
3. Once pasta is cooked, transfer to a serving bowl. Pour cheese mixture on top. Toss to combine.
4. Serve warm.

Calories 319,
Total fat 17 g,
Carbs 28 g,
Protein 17 g,

Macaroni Grill's Pasta Milano

Difficulty ●○○

Cost $ $ $

Servings 6

Preparation Time............. 5 min

Cooking Time.................... 20 min

- 1 pound bowtie pasta
- 2 teaspoons olive oil
- 1 pound chicken, chopped into small pieces
- 1 12-ounce package mushrooms, chopped
- 1 cup onion, minced
- 2 garlic cloves, finely minced
- 1/2 cup sun dried tomatoes, diced
- 1 1/2 cups half and half

- 1 tablespoon butter, softened
- 1/2 cup Parmesan cheese, shredded, plus some more for serving
- 1 teaspoon black pepper, ground
- 1 tablespoon fresh basil, minced

1. Follow instructions on package to cook bowtie pasta. Drain, then set aside.
2. Add oil to a pan over medium-high heat. Once hot, add chicken and stir-fry for about 5 to 6 minutes until cooked through. Set chicken aside onto a plate.
3. In the same pan, toss in mushrooms, onions, garlic, and sun dried tomatoes. Sauté until onions turn soft and mushrooms become a light brown, then sprinkle salt and pepper to season. Return chicken to pan and mix.
4. Mix half and half, butter, Parmesan, pepper, and basil in a small bowl.
5. Add half and half mixture to pan. Stir, and let simmer for about 3 to 4 minutes or until pan ingredients are thoroughly heated. Mix in pasta until coated well.

Calories 600,
Total fat 18 g,
Carbs 69 g,
Protein 42 g,

Olive Garden's Fettuccine Alfredo

Difficulty ●○○

Cost $ $ $

Servings 6

Preparation Time............ 5 min

Cooking Time................... 25 min

- 1/2 cup butter, melted
- 2 tablespoons cream cheese
- 1 pint heavy cream
- 1 teaspoon garlic powder
- Some salt
- Some black pepper
- 2/3 cup parmesan cheese, grated
- 1 pound fettuccine, cooked

1. Melt the cream cheese in the melted butter over medium heat until soft.
2. Add the heavy cream and season the mixture with garlic powder, salt, and pepper.
3. Reduce the heat to low and allow the mixture to simmer for another 15 to 20 minutes.
4. Remove the mixture from heat and add in the parmesan. Stir everything to melt the cheese.
5. Pour the sauce over the pasta and serve.

Calories: 767.3
Fat: 52.9 g
Carbs: 57.4 g
Protein: 17.2 g

Red Lobster's Shrimp Pasta

Difficulty ●●○

Cost $ $ $

Servings 4

Preparation Time............ 5 min

Cooking Time.................. 30 min

- 8 ounces linguini or spaghetti pasta
- 1/3 cup extra virgin olive oil
- 3 garlic cloves
- 1 pound shrimp, peeled, deveined
- 2/3 cup clam juice or chicken broth

- 1/3 cup white wine
- 1 cup heavy cream

1. Cook the Pasta according to package directions. Simmer the garlic in hot oil over low heat, until tender. Increase the heat to low to medium and add the shrimp. When the shrimp is
2. Cooked, transfer it to a separate bowl along with the garlic. Keep the remaining oil in the pan. Pour the clam or chicken broth into the pan and bring to a boil.
3. Add the wine and adjust the heat to medium. Keep cooking the mixture for another 3 minutes. While stirring the mixture, reduce the heat to low and add in the cream and cheese. Keep stirring. When the mixture thickens, return the shrimp to the pan and throw in the remaining ingredients (except the pasta). Place the pasta in a bowl and pour the sauce over it. Mix everything together and serve. Garnish with parsley and parmesan cheese, if desired

Calories. 590
Fat: 26 g
Carbs: 54 g
Protein: 34 g

Olive Garden's Steak Gorgonzola

Difficulty ● ● ○

Cost $ $ $

Servings 6

Preparation Time............ 5 min

Cooking Time.................. 90 min

Pasta:
- 1/2 pounds boneless beef top sirloin steaks, cut into 1/2-inch cubes
- 1 pound fettucine or linguini, cooked
- 2 tablespoons sun-dried tomatoes, chopped
- 2 tablespoons balsamic vinegar glaze
- Some fresh parsley leaves, chopped

Marinade:
- 1/2 cups Italian dressing
- 1 tablespoon fresh rosemary, chopped
- 1 tablespoon fresh lemon juice (optional)
- Spinach Gorgonzola Sauce:
- 4 cups baby spinach, trimmed
- 2 cups Alfredo sauce (recipe follows)
- 1/2 cup green onion, chopped
- 6 tablespoons gorgonzola, crumbled, and divided)

1. Cook the pasta and set aside. Mix together the marinade ingredients in a
2. Sealable container.
3. Marinate the beef in the container for an hour.
4. While the beef is marinating, make the Spinach Gorgonzola sauce. Heat the Alfredo sauce in a saucepan over medium heat. Add spinach and green onions. Let simmer until the spinach wilt. Crumble 4 tablespoons of the Gorgonzola cheese on top of the sauce. Let melt and stir. Set aside remaining 2 tablespoons of the cheese for garnish. Set aside and cover with lid to keep warm.
5. When the beef is done marinating, grill each piece depending on your preference.
6. Toss the cooked pasta and the Alfredo sauce in a saucepan, and then transfer to a plate.
7. Top the pasta with the beef, and garnish with balsamic glaze, sun-dried tomatoes, crumble gorgonzola cheese, and parsley leaves.
8. Serve and enjoy.

Calories: 740.5
Fat: 27.7 g
Carbs: 66 g
Protein: 54.3 g

Cheesecake Factory's Pasta di Vinci

Difficulty ● ● ●

Cost $ $ $

Servings 4

Preparation Time............ 10 min

Cooking Time.................. 50 min

- 1/2 red onion, chopped
- 1 cup mushrooms, quartered
- 2 teaspoons garlic, chopped
- 1 pound chicken breast, cut into bite-size pieces
- 3 tablespoons butter, divided
- 2 tablespoons flour
- 2 teaspoons salt
- 1/4 cup white wine
- 1 cup cream of chicken soup mixed with some milk
- 4 tablespoons heavy cream
- Basil leaves for serving, chopped Parmesan cheese for serving
- 1 pound penne pasta, cooked, drained

1. Sauté the onion, mushrooms and garlic in 1 tablespoon of the butter.
2. When they are tender, remove them from the butter and place in a bowl. Cook the chicken in the same pan. When the chicken is done, transfer it to the bowl containing the garlic, onions, and mushrooms, and set everything aside.
3. Using the same pan, make a roux using the flour and remaining butter over low to medium heat. When the roux is ready, mix in the salt, wine, and cream of chicken mixture. Continue stirring the mixture, making sure that it does not burn. When the mixture thickens and allow the mixture to simmer for a few more minutes. Mix in the ingredients that you set aside, and transfer the cooked pasta to a bowl or plate. Pour the sauce over the pasta, garnish with parmesan cheese and basil, and serve.

Calories: 844.9
Fat: 35.8 g
Carbs: 96.5 g
Protein: 33.9 g

Longhorn Steakhouse's Mac & Cheese

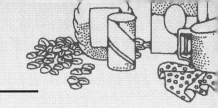

Difficulty ●○○

Cost $ $ $

Servings 10

Preparation Time............ 20 min

Cooking Time.................. 20 min

- 1 pound cavatappi pasta, cooked
- 2 tablespoons butter
- 2 tablespoons flour
- 2 cups half-and-half
- 2 ounces gruyere cheese, shredded
- 8 ounces white cheddar, shredded
- 2 tablespoons parmesan cheese, shredded
- 4 ounces fontina cheese, shredded
- 1 teaspoon smoked paprika
- 4 pieces bacon, crispy, crumbled
- 1/2 cup panko bread crumbs

1. Make a roux by cooking the melted butter and flour over medium heat.
2. When the roux is cooked, add in the half-and-half 1/2 cup at a time, adding more as the sauce thickens.
3. Slowly add the rest of the ingredients (except the pasta) one at a time, really allowing each ingredient to incorporate itself into the sauce. Continue stirring the mixture until everything is heated.
4. Place the pasta in a greased 13×9 baking pan or 6 individual baking dishes and pour the sauce over it. Sprinkle the bacon and panko bread crumbs over the top of the pasta.
5. Bake the pasta in an oven preheated to 350 Fahrenheit for 20-25 minutes, or until breadcrumbs start to become golden brown.
6. Let the pasta cool, and serve.

Calories: 610
Fat: 37 g
Carbs: 43 g
Protein: 26 g

Soups and Stews

O' Charley Loaded Potato Soup

Difficulty ●○○

Cost $ $ $

Servings 6-8

Preparation Time............ 10 min

Cooking Time................... 50 min

- 3 pounds red potatoes
- 1/4 cup melted margarine
- 1/4 cup flour
- 8 cups half-and-half
- 1 (16-ounce) block melted Velveeta cheese

- Garlic powder, to taste
- 1 teaspoon hot pepper sauce
- 1/2 pound crispy fried bacon
- 1/2 cup shredded Cheddar cheese
- 1/2 cup chopped fresh parsley
- 1/2 cup chopped fresh chives

1. Peel and dice the potatoes into 1/2 cubes. Place it in a large stockpot then cover with water. Boil for 10 minutes. In a separate soup pot, combine margarine and flour over low heat. Stir constantly, gradually adding the half-and-half, until the liquid begins to thicken. Add the Velveeta and stir well. Drain the potatoes and add to cream mixture.

2. Stir in hot pepper sauce and garlic powder. Cover and cook over low heat for 30 minutes, stirring occasionally. Place into individual serving bowls and top with crumbled bacon, Cheddar, parsley, and chives.

Calories 470;
Fat 17g;
Carbs 44g;
Protein 12g

Olive Garden Angel Hair and Three Onion Soup

Difficulty ●○○

Cost $ $ $

Servings 6

Preparation Time............ 15 min

Cooking Time.................... 40 min

- 1/2 pound pearl onions
- 1 medium thinly sliced red onion
- 1 medium thinly sliced Vidalia onion
- 4 tablespoons olive oil
- 6 cups chicken stock
- Salt, to taste

- 1/4 teaspoon red pepper flakes
- 1/2 pound angel hair pasta, broken in 2" pieces
- 1/4 cup chopped Italian parsley
- 4 teaspoons grated Romano Cheese

1. Place the onions and oil in a large saucepan over low heat and sauté, stirring occasionally, for about 20 minutes, until the onions are soft. Add the stock, salt, and pepper flakes and simmer for about 1 hour. Add the pasta and parsley and cook until pasta is al dente. Sprinkle with grated Romano cheese.

Calories 526;
Fat 20g;
Carbs 68g;
Protein 19g

Olive Garden Chicken and Gnocchi Soup

Difficulty ● ○ ○

Cost $ $ $

Servings 6-8

Preparation Time............ 20 min

Cooking Time.................. 20 min

- 1/3 cup butter
- 2 cloves minced garlic
- 1 pound cubed chicken
- 1/3 cup flour
- Cracked pepper, to taste
- 2 cups whole milk

- 2 cups heavy cream
- 1/2 shredded carrot
- 1 stalk celery shredded
- 1/4 cup shredded onion
- 1/2 cup torn fresh spinach
- 3 chicken bouillon cubes
- 1 (16-ounce) package frozen gnocchi

1. Melt the butter then sauté the garlic in a soup pot on medium heat for 2-3 minutes.
2. Add the chicken and cook 8-10 minutes until done. Stir in the flour and pepper and mix well, cook for 2-3 minutes, until the flour is cooked into the chicken. Add the milk and heavy cream.
3. Add the carrots, celery, onion, and spinach. Drop 3 bouillon cubes into the pot. Mix ingredients well, stirring occasionally. Cover and simmer for 10 minutes. Add the frozen gnocchi to the pot.
4. Cook 3-4 minutes more, until the gnocchi is done.

Calories 230;
Fat 12g;
Carbs 22g;
Protein 11g

Olive Garden Minestrone Soup

Difficulty ●○○

Cost $ $ $

Servings 6-8

Preparation Time............ 15 min

Cooking Time................... 25 min

- 3 tablespoons olive oil
- 1/4 cup minced celery
- 4 cloves minced garlic
- 1 small minced onion
- 1/2 cup frozen Italian-style green beans
- 1/2 cup chopped zucchini
- 4 cups vegetable broth
- 2 (15-ounce) cans drained red kidney beans
- 2 (15-ounce) cans drained small white bean
- 1/2 cup shredded carrots

- 1 (14-ounce) can diced tomatoes, drained
- 3 cups hot water
- 2 tablespoons minced fresh parsley
- 1 1/2 teaspoons dried oregano
- 1 1/2 teaspoons salt
- 1/2 teaspoon pepper
- 1/2 teaspoon dried basil
- 1/4 teaspoon dried thyme
- 4 cups fresh baby spinach
- 1/2 cup small shell pasta

1. Add the olive oil in a large soup pot and heat it over medium heat. Sauté the celery, garlic, onion, green beans, and zucchini for 5 minutes

2. Add the broth, beans, carrots, drained tomatoes, hot water, and spices. Bring the soup to a boil. Reduce heat and simmer for 20 minutes. Add spinach leaves and pasta. Cook for an additional 20 minutes.

Calories 300;
Fat 1g;
Carbs 17g;
Protein 5g

Olive Garden Pasta Roma Soup

Difficulty ● ○ ○

Cost $ $ $

Servings 6-8

Preparation Time............ 10 min

Cooking Time.................. 30 min

- 2 (16-ounce) cans drained garbanzo beans
- 1/3 cup olive oil
- 1 cup julienned carrots
- ¾ cup diced onions
- 1 cup diced celery
- 1/4 teaspoon minced garlic
- 6 slices cooked bacon
- 1 1/2 cups canned drained chopped tomatoes

- 1 quart chicken broth
- 1/2 teaspoon black pepper
- 1/8 teaspoon ground rosemary
- 2 tablespoons chopped fresh parsley
- 1/2 cup cooked macaroni

1. In a food processor, add the beans then pulse on and off until the beans are mashed well. Heat the oil in a large soup pot. Add the carrots, onions, celery, and garlic and sauté for 5 minutes on medium heat.
2. Add the remaining ingredients except pasta to the pot. Bring everything to a boil. Simmer and cook it in a low heat for 20 minutes, stirring occasionally. Add the pasta to the finished soup and serve immediately.
3.

Calories 595;
Fat 27.5g;
Carbs 66.3g;
Protein 22.9g

Olive Garden Seafood Pasta Chowder

Difficulty ●○○

Cost $ $ $

Servings 6-8

Preparation Time............ 10 min

Cooking Time.................. 20 min

- 6 ounces small shells or bowtie pasta
- 3 ounces crab meat
- 6 tablespoons butter
- 1/2 pound sliced fresh mushrooms
- 2 (1-ounce) packages Newburg sauce
- 3 cups milk
- 1 1/2 cups water
- 1/4 cup dry white wine
- 1/4 cup sliced green onions

1. Cook the pasta by following the package instructions. Sort the crab meat to remove any shell pieces. Melt the butter in a 3-quart sauce pan. Add the mushrooms and sauté for 3 minutes. Add the Newburg sauce and stir well. Add the milk, water, and wine and stir well until the mixture comes to a boil. Reduce heat and simmer 5-8 minutes, stirring constantly. Add the green onions, pasta, and crab. Stir to combine and heat another 5-10 minutes.

Calories 214;
Fat 25g;
Carbs 16g;
Protein 10g

Olive Garden Zuppa Toscana Soup

Difficulty ● ○ ○

Cost $ $ $

Servings 6-8

Preparation Time............ 20 min

Cooking Time.................... 45 min

- 1 pound Italian sausage, crumbled
- 1/2 pound smoked bacon, chopped
- 1 large chopped onion
- 2 large diced russet baking potatoes
- 2 (14.5-ounce) cans chicken broth
- 1 quart water
- 2 cloves minced garlic
- Salt and pepper, to taste
- 2 cups chopped kale or Swiss chard
- 1 cup heavy whipping cream

1. Cook the sausage in a 300°F oven for approximately 30 minutes. Drain on paper towels.
2. Brown bacon in a small skillet over medium-high heat
3. Drain on paper towels.
4. Place the onions, potatoes, broth, water, and garlic in a soup pot.
5. Cook on medium heat for 15 minutes, or until the potatoes are done
6. Add the sausage and bacon. Sprinkle in salt and pepper to taste.
7. Simmer for another 10 minutes. Turn to low heat. Add the kale and cream.
8. Heat another 5-10 minutes.

Calories 220;
Fat 15g;
Carbs 15g;
Protein 7g

Chang Wonton Soup

Difficulty ●○○

Cost $ $ $

Servings 10-12

Preparation Time............ 15 min

Cooking Time.................... 45 min

For the Soup
- 4 cups chicken stock
- 2 cubed chicken breast halves without skin
- 1 pound peeled medium shrimp
- 1 cup torn fresh spinach
- 1 cup sliced mushrooms
- 1 (8-ounce) can drained water chestnuts
- 1 teaspoon light brown sugar
- 1 teaspoon finely chopped fresh ginger
- 2 tablespoons soy sauce
- 1 teaspoon finely chopped green onion
- 1 tbsp. of dry or sherry Chinese rice wine

For the Homemade Wontons:
- 8 coarsely chopped medium shrimp
- 1/2 pound pork, coarsely chopped
- 1 teaspoon light brown sugar
- 1 teaspoon finely chopped fresh ginger
- 2 tablespoons soy sauce
- 1 teaspoon finely chopped green onion
- 1 tbsp. of dry sherry or Chinese rice wine
- 24 wonton wrappers

1. Rolling boil the chicken stock then add the remaining ingredients. Next, add the chicken in the soup cook it for about 10 minutes. When making the homemade wontons, mix the pork and shrimp with brown sugar, rice wine, soy sauce, green onions, and ginger in a large bowl. Blend well and set aside for 25-30 minutes for the flavors to blend.

2. Have 1 teaspoon of the filling in the center of each wonton wrapper. With a little water, wet the edges of each wonton and press them together with your fingers to seal. Fold each wonton over.

3. To cook, add wontons to boiling chicken stock and cook for 4-5 minutes. Transfer to individual soup bowls and serve garnished with thinly sliced green onions.

Calories 60;
Fat 1g;
Carbs 8g;
Protein 4g

Red Lobster Clam Chowder

Difficulty ●○○

Cost $ $ $

Servings 6-8

Preparation Time........... 5 min

Cooking Time................... 30 min

- 2 tablespoons butter
- 1/4 teaspoon chopped garlic
- 1 cup diced onions
- 1/2 cup diced celery
- 1/2 cup diced leeks
- 2 tablespoons flour
- 4 cups milk

- 1 cup minced clams with juice
- 1 cup diced potatoes
- 1 tablespoon salt
- 1 teaspoon thyme
- 1/2 cup heavy cream

1. In a soup pot, melt the butter in a medium heat and then sauté the onion, garlic, leeks, and celery for 3-4 minutes. Next, remove from the heat then add flour. Mix. Return it to the stove. Add the milk then stir. Drain the clams then add the juice to the soup.

2. Bring to a boil, stir it often. Simmer it by reducing the heat. Add seasonings and the potatoes.

3. Simmer it again for 10 minutes. Add the clams then simmer for 5-8 minutes.

4. Finish by adding the heavy cream.

Calories 250;
Fat 16g;
Carbs 20g;
Protein 7g

Ruby Tuesday White Chicken Chili

Difficulty ●●○

Cost $ $ $

Servings 8

Preparation Time........... 10 min

Cooking Time................... 2 h

- 1 pound great northern beans
- 6 cups chicken stock
- 2 medium chopped onions
- 2 minced garlic cloves
- 6 cups diced cooked chicken
- 1 cup salsa
- 2 seeded and diced jalapeño peppers
- 2 diced chili peppers

- 1 1/2 teaspoons oregano
- 2 teaspoons cumin
- 1/4 teaspoon cayenne pepper
- 1 tablespoon vegetable oil
- Salt, to taste

1. Soak beans in water overnight. Drain the beans the next day. In a large stock pot, add the chicken stock, beans and half the onions and garlic.

2. Simmer for 2 hours until the beans become soft, stir it frequently. Add the salsa and chicken.

3. Sauté spices, peppers and the remaining garlic and onions in oil for 3-4 minutes in a large skillet. Add the chili, salt and pepper to the pot. Simmer it for 1 more hour.

Calories 250;
Fat 16g;
Carbs 20g;
Protein 7g

T.G.I. Friday Broccoli Cheese Soup

Difficulty ●○○

Cost $ $ $

Servings 8

Preparation Time............ 5 min

Cooking Time.................. 30 min

- 4 cups chicken broth
- 1 cup half-and-half
- 1 cup water
- 4 slices American cheese
- 1/2 cup flour
- 1/2 teaspoon dried onion flakes
- 1/4 teaspoon black pepper
- 4 1/2 cups bite-size broccoli florets

1. Combine all the ingredients except the broccoli into a large soup pot. Bring to a boil, stirring constantly. Reduce to a simmer. Add the broccoli and simmer for 15 minutes, or until the broccoli is tender. Garnish with shredded Cheddar cheese.

Calories 250;
Fat 16g;
Carbs 20g;
Protein 7g

T.G.I. Friday French Onion Soup

Difficulty ●○○

Cost $ $ $

Servings 4

Preparation Time............ 5 min

Cooking Time.................. 30 min

- 2 tablespoons butter
- 4 medium sliced onions
- 4 cups beef broth
- 1 tablespoon Worcestershire sauce
- 1/4 teaspoon black pepper
- Dash of dried thyme
- 1 cup French bread cubes
- 1/2 cup shredded mozzarella cheese

1. Melt butter in a 2-quart saucepan. Add the onions and cook 20 minutes, stirring occasionally. Add the broth, Worcestershire sauce, pepper, and thyme. Increase the heat to medium-high and bring to a boil. Reduce the heat to low, cover, and simmer for 5 minutes. Divide soup into 4 individual serving crocks. Place the bread cubes on top of the soup and then add the cheese. Put the soup bowls under the broiler to melt the cheese until it turns slightly brown.

Calories 310;
Fat 27g;
Carbs 14g;
Protein 6g

PF Chang Spicy Chicken Noodle Soup

Difficulty ● ○ ○

Cost $ $ ○

Servings 4-6

Preparation Time............ 15 min

Cooking Time................... 15 min

- 2 quarts chicken stock
- 1 tablespoon granulated sugar
- 3 tablespoons white vinegar
- 2 cloves garlic, minced
- 1 tablespoon ginger, freshly minced
- 1/4 cup of soy sauce
- Sriracha sauce to taste
- Red pepper flakes to taste

- 1 lbs. Boneless chicken breast, cut into thin 2-3 inch pieces
- 3 tablespoons cornstarch
- Salt to taste
- 1 cup mushrooms, sliced
- 1 cup grape tomatoes, halved
- 3 green onions, sliced
- 2 tablespoons fresh cilantro, chopped
- 1/2 pound pasta, cooked to just under package directions and drained

1. Add the chicken stock, sugar, vinegar, garlic, ginger, soy sauce, Sriracha and red pepper flakes to a large saucepan. Boil it and then lower the heat to a simmer. Let cook for 5 minutes.

2. Season chicken with salt to taste. In a resalable bag, combine the chicken and the cornstarch. Shake to coat. Add the chicken to the simmering broth a piece at a time. Then add the mushrooms. Continue to cook for another 5 minutes.

3. Stir in the tomatoes, green onions, cilantro, and cooked pasta. Serve with additional cilantro.

Calories 500;
Protein 32g;
Fat 8g;
Carbs: 73g

Panera Broccoli Cheddar Soup

Difficulty ● ○ ○

Cost $ $ $

Servings 8

Preparation Time............ 15 min

Cooking Time.................... 50 min

- 1 tablespoon butter
- 1/2 onion, diced
- 1/4 cup melted butter
- 1/4 cup flour
- 2 cups of milk
- 2 cups chicken stock
- 1 1/2 cup broccoli florets, diced

- 1 cup carrots, cut into thin strips
- 1 stalk celery, sliced
- 2 1/2 cups Cheddar cheese, grated
- Salt and pepper, to taste

1. Melt tablespoon of butter in a frying pan and cook onion over medium heat for 5 minutes or until caramelized. Set aside. In a saucepan, mix melted butter and flour, then cook on medium-low heat. Add 1 or 2 tablespoons milk to the flour to prevent from burning—Cook for at least 3 minutes or until smooth.

2. Gently pour the rest of the milk in with the flour while stirring. Mix in chicken stock. Simmer for 20 minutes or until thick and well blended. Toss in the broccoli, carrots, cooked onion, and celery. Cook for an additional 20 minutes or until vegetables turns soft. Mix in cheese and stir until the cheese is completely melted—season with salt and pepper, to taste. Transfer into individual bowls. Serve.

Calories 304;
Fat 23g;
Carbs 11g;
Protein 14g

Outback Walkabout Soup

Difficulty ●○○

Cost $ $ $

Servings 4

Preparation Time............ 10 min

Cooking Time................... 50 min

- Thick white Sauce
- 3 tablespoons butter
- 3 tablespoons flour
- 1/4 teaspoon salt
- 1 1/2 cups whole milk
- Soup
- 2 cups yellow sweet onions, thinly sliced
- 3 tablespoons butter

- 1 can (14.5 ounces) chicken broth
- 1/2 teaspoon salt
- 1/4 teaspoon fresh ground black pepper
- 2 chicken bouillon cubes
- 1/4 cup Velveeta cubes, diced, packed
- 1 1/2-1¾ cups white sauce (recipe above)
- Cheddar cheese for garnish, shredded
- Crusty bread for serving

1. Make the thick white sauce first. Make a roux by cooking melted butter and flour over medium heat. Slowly pour the milk onto the roux, a little at a time, while constantly stirring the mixture. When the mixture reaches a pudding-like consistency, remove it from heat and set aside. In a soup pot, sauté the onions in the butter over medium heat until they become translucent.

2. Add the rest of the ingredients, except the cheese and white sauce, to the pot and mix everything together. When the mixture has heated up completely, add the cheese and white sauce. Bring the entire mixture to a simmer on medium-low heat. Continuously stir the soup until everything is completely mixed together.

3. When the cheese has melted, turn the heat lower and continue to cook the soup for another 30 to 45 minutes. Ladle the soup into bowls and garnish with cheese. Serve with a side of bread.

Calories 329,
Fat 25 g,
Carbs 17g,
Protein 6 g

Chevy Chipotle Slaw

Difficulty ● ○ ○

Cost $ $ $

Servings 6

Preparation Time............ 10 min

Cooking Time.................. /

- 3 cups finely shredded white cabbage
- 3 cups finely shredded red cabbage
- ¾ cup Sweet Chipotle Dressing
- Sweet Chipotle Dressing
- 1 tablespoon diced onion
- 2 teaspoons minced garlic
- 1 chipotle pepper in adobo sauce, diced

- 1 tablespoon adobo sauce
- 2 tablespoons mustard
- 1/2 teaspoon ground cumin
- 1/2 cup diced fresh tomatoes
- 2 tablespoons chopped cilantro
- 2/3Cup of seasoned rice wine vinegar
- 1/4 teaspoon black pepper
- 1 teaspoon salt
- 2 tablespoons honey
- 1/2 cup olive oil

1. Shred the cabbage. Put it in a large bowl. Combine all the dressing ingredients EXCEPT the oil until smooth in a blender or food processor.
2. While the blender is running, drizzle in the oil to make an emulsion.
3. Pour ¾ cup of the dressing over the cabbage and toss to coat.
4. Put the remaining dressing in an airtight container and store it in the fridge for up to 1 week.

Calories 100;
Protein 1g;
Fat 10g;
Carbs 6g

Café Rio Black Beans

Difficulty ●○○

Cost $ $ $

Servings 8

Preparation Time............ 10 min

Cooking Time................... 30 min

- 2 tablespoons olive oil
- 3 cloves garlic, minced
- 1 jalapeño pepper, minced
- 2 (15-ounce) cans black beans (one can drain, one with liquid)
- 2 teaspoons cumin
- 12 ounces tomato juice
- 1 teaspoon salt
- 1/2 teaspoon black pepper
- 1/4 cup chopped cilantro

1. In a large non-stick skillet over medium heat, warm the oil and sauté the garlic and jalapeño until fragrant. Add the beans and cumin. Bring the mixture to a simmer for 5-10 minutes, until some of the liquid has evaporated. Stir in the tomato juice, salt, pepper, and cilantro. Cook to heat through, and serve.

Calories 153;
Protein 9g;
Fat 3g;
Carbs 25g

Applebee Cheese Chicken Tortilla Soup

Difficulty ●○○

Cost $ $ $

Servings 6-8

Preparation Time............ 10 min

Cooking Time.................. 40 min

- 2 tablespoons vegetable oil
- 2 teaspoons minced garlic
- 1 medium chopped onion
- 1/4 cup chopped green pepper
- 1 (15 ounces) can tomato purée
- 4 cups chicken stock
- 1 teaspoon sugar
- 1/2 teaspoon salt
- 1 teaspoon chili powder

- 1 teaspoon Worcestershire sauce
- 10 (6") yellow corn tortillas
- 4 tablespoons flour
- 1/2 cup of water
- 1-pound cooked chicken
- 1 cup cream
- 1/4 cup nonfat sour cream
- 8 ounces Velveeta cheese, cut into 1" cubes

1. Add oil and sauté garlic, onions, and green peppers in a large stockpot over medium heat. Add chicken stock, tomato purée, sugar, salt, chili powder, and Worcestershire sauce to the pot.

2. Bring to a boil, reduce the heat and simmer for 20 minutes. Cut tortillas into 1/4" strips and bake in the oven at 400°F for 6-8 minutes until crispy.

3. In a small bowl, mix flour and water, then whisk into the soup. Add chicken and cream, bring to a boil, and then simmer for 5 minutes. Put it into bowls and garnish with the cheese, sour cream, and tortilla strips.

Calories 190
Protein 9g;
Fat 9g;
Carbs 18g

California Pizza Kitchen
Pea and Barley Soup

Difficulty ●○○

Cost $ $

Servings 8

Preparation Time............ 10 min

Cooking Time.................... 40 min

- 2 cups split peas
- 6 cups of water
- 4 cups chicken broth
- 1/3 cup minced onion
- 1 large clove minced garlic
- 2 teaspoons lemon juice
- 1 teaspoon salt
- 1 teaspoon granulated sugar
- 1/4 teaspoon dried parsley

- 1/4 teaspoon white pepper
- Dash dried thyme
- 1/2 cup barley
- 6 cups of water
- 2 medium diced carrots
- 1/2 stalk diced celery

1. Rinse and drain the split peas and add them to a large pot with 6 cups of water, chicken broth, onion, garlic, lemon juice, salt, sugar, parsley, pepper, and thyme. Bring to a boil. Reduce heat and simmer for 75 minutes, or until the peas becomes soft.

2. Combine the barley with 6 cups of water in a saucepan while the peas are cooking. Bring to a boil, reduce heat, and simmer for 75 minutes, or until the barley is soft and most of the water has been absorbed.

3. Drain the barley in a colander and add it to the split peas. Add the celery and carrots and continue to simmer the soup for 15-30 minutes, or until the carrots are tender. Stir occasionally. Turn off the heat, cover the soup, and let it sit for 10-15 minutes

Calories 340;
Protein 66g;
Fat 23g;
Carbs 3g

Outback's Baked Potato Soup

Difficulty ● ● ●

Cost $ $ $

Servings 8

Preparation Time............ 5 min

Cooking Time................... 40 min

- 2 quarts water
- 8 medium-sized potatoes, cut into chunks
- 4 cans of chicken broth
- 1 small onion, minced
- 1 teaspoon salt
- 1 teaspoon of ground pepper
- 2 cups of cold water
- 1 cup of butter

- ¾ cup of flour
- 1 1/2 cup of heavy cream
- 1 1/2 cups of jack cheese
- 2-3 thick-cut bacon slices, cooked and diced
- 1/4 cup of green onion, minced

1. In a pot, add water and potatoes. Bring back a boil, reduce heat to medium, and cook potatoes for 10-15 minutes or tender. Drain and put aside.

2. In a separate pot, pour in broth and blend in onions, salt, pepper, and water. Simmer for 20 minutes.

3. Meanwhile, in another pot, whisk together butter and flour. Slowly add this to the pan of broth. Stir in cream to the mixture and simmer for 20 minutes. Mix in potatoes to reheat.

4. Sprinkle jack cheese, bacon bits, and green onions on top. Serve.

Calories: 845,
Total Fat: 49 g,
Carbs: 81 g,
Protein: 23 g,

Applebee's Tomato Basil Soup

Difficulty ● ○ ○

Cost $ $ $

Servings 8

Preparation Time............ 10 min

Cooking Time................... 20 min

- 3 tablespoons of olive oil
- 1 small garlic clove, finely chopped
- 1 10 ¾-ounce can condense tomato soup
- 1/4 cup of bottled marinara sauce
- 5 ounces of water
- 1 teaspoon of fresh oregano, diced

- 1/2 teaspoon of ground black pepper
- 1 tablespoon of fresh basil, diced
- 6 Italian-style seasoned croutons
- 2 tablespoons of Parmesan cheese, shredded

1. Heat oil in a pan over medium heat. Add garlic and fry for two to three minutes or until garlic is soft and aromatic.
2. Pour tomato soup and marinara sauce into pan and stir and add water gradually. Then add oregano and pepper and once simmering, reduce heat to low. Cook for about 15 more minutes until all the flavors are combined. Add basil and stir.
3. Transfer to bowls. Add croutons on top and sprinkle with Parmesan cheese.
4. Serve.

Calories 350,
Total fat 26 g,
Carbs 28 g,
Protein 6 g,

Chicken Enchilada Soup from Chili's

Difficulty ● ○ ○

Cost $ $ $

Servings 8

Preparation Time............ 10 min

Cooking Time.................. 20 min

- 1-pound of chicken breast, boneless and skinless, cut in half
- 1 tablespoon of vegetable oil
- 1/2 cup of onion, chopped
- 1 garlic clove, finely chopped
- 1-quart chicken broth
- 1 cup of masa harina

- 3 cups of water, divided
- 1 cup of enchilada sauce
- 2 cups of cheddar cheese, grated
- 1 teaspoon of salt
- 1 teaspoon of chili powder
- 1/2 teaspoon of ground cumin
- Crispy tortilla strips for garnish

It's quick, easy, tastes fantastic, and you can store it in the fridge and heat it again later... What more could you ask from a soup?

1. Heat oil in a pot over medium heat. Add chicken breasts and evenly cook until browned on all sides. Remove from pot. Shred, then put aside.
2. Return pot to heat and add onion and garlic. Sauté until onions are translucent. Add chicken stock.
3. Mix masa harina and a couple of cups water in a bowl, then add in the pot with the onions and garlic. Add the remaining water, enchilada sauce, cheddar, salt, flavorer, and cumin. Bring mixture to a boil.
4. Add cooked chicken to the pot and lower heat. Simmer for about 30 to 40 minutes until soup is thick.
5. Garnish with crispy tortilla strips and serve.

Calories: 290,
Total fat: 16 g,
Carbs: 14 g,
Protein: 22 g,

P.F. Chang's Chef John's Chicken Lettuce Wraps

Difficulty ●○○

Cost $ $ $

Servings 8

Preparation Time............ 10 min

Cooking Time.................... 20 min

- 1 1/2 pounds of skinless, boneless chicken thighs, coarsely chopped
- 1 can (8 ounces) of water chestnuts, drained, minced
- 1 cup of shiitake mushroom caps, diced
- 1/2 cup of yellow onion, minced
- 1/3 cup of green onion, chopped
- 1 tablespoon of soy sauce
- 1 tablespoon of ginger, freshly grated
- 2 teaspoons of brown sugar
- 2 tablespoons of vegetable oil
- Glaze:
- 1/4 cup of chicken stock

- 1/4 cup of rice wine vinegar
- 4 cloves garlic, minced
- 1 tablespoon of ketchup
- 1 tablespoon of soy sauce
- 2 teaspoons of sesame oil
- 2 teaspoons of brown sugar
- 1/2 teaspoon of red pepper flakes
- 1/2 teaspoon of dry mustard Herbs and Wrap:
- 1 1/2 tablespoons of fresh cilantro, chopped
- 1 1/2 tablespoons of fresh basil, chopped
- 1 1/2 tablespoons of green onion, chopped
- 16 leaves of iceberg lettuce, or as needed

If you are in the mood for a healthier snack, here's P.F. Chang's chicken lettuce wraps. It's filling and tasty!

1. Mix all the chicken mix ingredients (except the oil) together in a bowl. Cover the bowl with wrapping and place it in the refrigerator.
2. Whisk all the glaze ingredients together until everything is mixed thoroughly.
3. When the glaze is prepared, cook the chicken mix ingredients in the oil over high heat.
4. After 2 minutes, when the chicken is cooked, pour half the glaze over the chicken mix. Continue cooking the whole mixture until the glaze caramelizes. This part could take 10 to fifteen minutes.
5. Reduce the warmth to medium to low, then add the remaining glaze to the mixture. Cook for around three more minutes, continually stirring.
6. Stir in the chopped herbs (i.e., cilantro, basil, and onion) and continue cooking until they're incorporated into the chicken mixture.
7. Transfer the chicken to a plate and serve with lettuce.

Calories: 290,
Total fat: 16 g,
Carbs: 14 g,
Protein: 22 g,

Disneyland's Monterey Clam Chowder

Difficulty ● ○ ○

Cost $ $ $

Servings 4

Preparation Time............ 15 min

Cooking Time.................. 60 min

- 5 tablespoons of butter
- 5 tablespoons of flour
- 2 tablespoons of vegetable oil
- 1 1/2 cups of potatoes (peeled, diced)
- 1/2 cup of onion, diced
- 1/2 cup of red pepper
- 1/2 cup of green pepper
- 1/2 cup of celery
- 2 1/4 cups of clam juice
- 1 1/2 cups of heavy cream

- 1 cup of clams, chopped
- 1 tablespoon of fresh thyme or 1/2 tablespoon of dried thyme
- 1/4-1/2 teaspoon of salt
- 1 pinch of white pepper
- 1/3 -1/2 teaspoon of Tabasco sauce
- 4 individual sourdough of round bread made into bowls
- Chives for garnish (optional)

Prepare a magical dish from the most magical place on earth. This clam chowder soup will take your taste buds on the ride of their lives.

1. Make a roux by mixing melted butter and flour over medium heat for 10 minutes. Flour burns quickly, so confirm to observe the mixture closely. Set the roux aside.
2. Sauté the potatoes, onions, pepper, and celery in the oil for 10 minutes employing a soup pot.
3. Whisk the other the ingredients, including the roux, into the soup pot, and convey the whole mixture to a boil.
4. After the mixture has boiled, reduce the warmth and let it simmer for an additional 5 minutes.
5. Season the soup as you wish with salt and pepper. To serve, ladle the soup evenly into the prepared bread bowls and sprinkle with fresh chives if desired.

Calories: 472.3,
Fat: 36.9 g,
Carbs: 27.4 g,
Protein: 9.3 g,

Apple Walnut Chicken Salad

Difficulty ●○○

Cost $ $$

Servings 4

Preparation Time............ 15 min

Cooking Time................... 60 min

- For the chicken
- 3 cups of water
- 1 tablespoon of salt
- 1/2 teaspoon of garlic powder
- 1/4 teaspoon of hickory-flavored liquid smoke
- 1 boneless chicken breast, pounded to a 1/2-inch thickness
- 1/2 teaspoon of ground black pepper
- 1 tablespoon of oil
- For the balsamic vinaigrette:
- 1/4 cup of red wine vinegar
- 3 tablespoons of granulated sugar
- 3 tablespoons of honey
- 1 tablespoon of Dijon mustard
- 1/2 teaspoon of salt
- 1 teaspoon of minced garlic
- 1 teaspoon of lemon juice
- 1/2 teaspoon of Italian seasoning

- 1/4 teaspoon of dried tarragon
- 1 Pinch of ground black pepper
- 1 cup of extra-virgin olive oil
- For the candied walnuts:
- 1 teaspoon of peanut oil
- 1 teaspoon of honey
- 2 tablespoons of granulated sugar
- 1/4 teaspoon of vanilla extract
- 1/8 teaspoon of salt
- A pinch of cayenne pepper
- ¾ cup of chopped walnuts
- For the salad:
- 4 cups of romaine lettuce, chopped
- 4 cups of red leaf lettuce, chopped
- 1 apple, diced
- 1/2 small red onion, sliced
- 1/2 cup of diced celery
- 1/4 cup of blue cheese, crumbled

For the chicken brine:
1. Mix the water, salt, garlic powder, and liquid smoke in a medium-sized bowl.
2. Add the chicken, cover, and refrigerate for a minimum of three hours.
3. For the balsamic vinaigrette
4. Whisk together all ingredients listed EXCEPT the oil.
5. Gradually pour in the oil while whisking. Refrigerate until able to serve.
6. For the candied walnuts
7. In a skillet, mix the groundnut oil, honey, sugar, vanilla, salt, and cayenne pepper, and cook over medium heat.
8. When the mixture starts to boil, add the walnuts and stir until the sugar begins to caramelize. Stir for 1 minute then pour onto a baking sheet covered with paper. Allow the nuts to chill.

For the salad:
1. Remove the chicken from the brine and pat it dry with a towel and season with black pepper.
2. Place the chicken on a hot grill. Grill for 3 to 4 minutes on all sides or until cooked through and juices run clear. Let it cool and slice it into strips.
3. In a salad bowl, combine the romaine lettuce, red leaf lettuce, apple, onion, celery, and bleu. Divide it onto plates and pour on some dressing. Top with sliced chicken and candied walnuts.
4. Refrigerate any unused dressing.

Cheesy Walkabout Soup

Difficulty ●○○

Cost $ $ $

Servings 4

Preparation Time............ 10 min

Cooking Time.................... 45 min

- 6 tablespoons of butter, divided
- 2 large sweet onions, thinly sliced
- 2 cups of low sodium chicken broth
- 1/4 teaspoon of ground black pepper
- 2 chicken bouillon cubes
- 3 tablespoons of flour

- 1/4 teaspoon of salt
- 1 1/2 cups of whole milk
- Pinch nutmeg
- 1/4 cup of Velveeta cheese, cubed

This recipe isn't your average cheese soup; the sweet onion brings it to a whole other level. Serve it for lunch on a cold day, or as a starter to a steak dinner, Outback style!

1. In a large pot or Dutch oven, melt half the butter over medium heat. Add the onions. Cook, occasionally stirring, until the onions are transparent but not browned.
2. Add the chicken stock, black pepper, and bouillon cubes. Mix well and cook on low to heat through.
3. In a separate saucepan, melt the remaining butter. Add the flour and salt and cook, constantly whisking, until smooth and lightly browned. Gradually whisk in the milk and cook over medium heat until it's very thick. Mix in the nutmeg.
4. Add the béchamel sauce to the onion soup mixture, alongside the Velveeta cubes. Stir gently over medium heat until the cheese is melted, and everything is combined.

Calories: 260
Total Fat: 19g
Carbs: 13g
Protein: 5g

Meal

Taco Bell's AM Crunch wrap

Difficulty ●○○

Cost $ $$

Servings 2

Preparation Time............ 30 min

Cooking Time................... 40 min

- Flour tortillas (2 large)
- Whisked eggs (3-4) + Milk (1 tbsp.)
- Shredded sharp cheddar cheese (2-4 tbsp.)
- Shredded hash browns (heaping .5 cup)
- Hot sauce mild your choice (4 tbsp.)
- Bacon (4 crispy)
- Cooking oil spray
- Taco Bell sauce

1. Lightly spritz a skillet using cooking oil spray and warm using the medium temperature setting.
2. Whisk and add the eggs, salt, and pepper into a skillet. Whisk until they are fluffy and set them aside.
3. Warm a skillet and heat the tortillas for about half of a minute. Prepare and close them, placing them in a skillet to cook for about 30 to 40 seconds using the medium temperature setting.
4. Serve with sauce as desired.

Calories: 255
Carbs: 16 gr.
Protein: 15 gt.
Fat: 14 gr.

Taco Bell's Cinnamon Delights

Difficulty ● ○ ○

Cost $ $ $

Servings 24

Preparation Time............ 30 min

Cooking Time................... 20 min

- Pillsbury™ refrigerated cinnamon rolls with icing (24 oz. can)
- Cinnamon (2 tsp.)
- Granulated sugar (.75 cup)
- Butter (.25 cup)
- Warmed caramel ice cream topping (.25 cup)
- Betty Crocker™ Rich & Creamy white frosting (.25 cup)

1. Heat the oven at 350° Fahrenheit. Prepare a baking tray using a layer of parchment baking paper. Open the rolls and slice each one into three pieces. Roll each one into a ball.
2. Add the butter to a small microwave-safe dish to melt. Whisk the sugar and cinnamon in another bowl.
3. Roll the dough balls through the butter, then the cinnamon and sugar. Arrange them on the baking tin. Bake them until nicely browned (ten min.) and cool for another ten minutes.
4. Warm the frosting for about ten seconds in the microwave to soften it slightly for piping. Scoop the filling into the piping bag.
5. Squirt in the frosting into the ball until it puffs. Garnish them using the sauce and serve.

Calories: 621
Protein: 0.1 gr.
Fat: 2.3 gr.
Carbs: 10.7 gr.

Taco Bell's Dressed Egg Taco

Difficulty ●○○

Cost $ $ $

Servings 8

Preparation Time............ 25 min

Cooking Time.................... 15 min

- Black beans (.33 cup)
- Pico de Gallo (.33 cup)
- Cubed avocado (.33 cup)
- Lime juice (1 tbsp.)
- Frozen thawed potatoes (1 cup)
- Bulk pork sausage (.5 lb.)
- Eggs (6 large)
- 2% milk (2 tbsp.)

- Monterey Jack shredded cheese (.5 cup)
- Warmed flour tortillas (8 @ 6-inches)
- Optional Fixings:
- Pico de Gallo
- Sour cream
- Freshly chopped cilantro

1. Rinse and drain the beans.
2. Gently mix the avocado, beans, Pico de Gallo, and lime juice.
3. In a large cast-iron or another heavy skillet, cook the potatoes and crumbled sausage using the medium temperature setting until the sausage is no longer pink (6-8 min.).
4. Whisk the eggs and milk. Pour them into the skillet, stirring over medium heat until the eggs are thickened, and no liquid egg remains.
5. Stir in the cheese.
6. Spoon the egg mixture into each of the tortillas, and top with the bean mixture. Garnish them to your liking.

Calories: 291
Protein: 13 gr.
Fat: 16 gr.
Carbs: 22 gr.

Taco Bell's Delicious Tacos

Difficulty ● ○ ○

Cost $ $ $

Servings 12

Preparation Time............ 25 min

Cooking Time................... 15 min

- Ground chuck (1.33 lb.)
- Golden Masa Harina corn flour. Bob's Red Mill (1.5 tbsp.)
- Chili powder (4.5 tsp.)
- Sugar (.25 tsp.)
- Ground cumin (.25 tsp.)
- Dried minced onion (1 tsp.)
- Spices @.5 tsp.
- Onion powder

- Seasoning salt
- Garlic powder
- Paprika
- Garlic salt
- Beef bouillon powder

To Serve:
- Taco shells (12)
- Shredded Iceberg lettuce (half of 1 head)
- Diced Roma tomatoes (2)
- Shredded cheddar cheese (1 cup)
- Optional: Sour cream

1. Combine all of the 'beef filling' fixings except for the meat. Combine the spice mix blending thoroughly.
2. Cook the beef in a skillet until browned. Transfer it from the burner and dump the meat into a strainer to rinse with hot water.
3. Toss the beef into the pan and stir in the spice mix with water (.75-1 cup). Simmer using the med-low temperature setting to cook away most of the liquids (20 min.)
4. Prepare the tacos. Pop the shells into a 350° Fahrenheit oven for 7-10 minutes.
5. Assemble them with the meat, lettuce, tomatoes, sour cream, and cheese to your liking.
6. Serve them promptly.

Calories: 236
Protein: 12 gr.
Fat: 15 gr.
Carbs: 10 gr.

Taco Bell's Chalupa Supreme

Difficulty ●○○

Cost $ $ $

Servings 6

Preparation Time............ 35 min

Cooking Time.................... 25 min

- Corn tortillas (6 @ 6-inches)
- Olive oil (2 tsp.)
- Shredded part-skim mozzarella cheese (.75 cup)
- Cooked chicken breast (2 cups)
- Diced tomatoes with green chiles (14.5 oz.)
- Ground cumin (1 tsp.)

- Garlic powder (1 tsp.)
- Black pepper and salt (.25 tsp. of each)
- Onion powder (1 tsp.)
- Finely shredded cabbage (5 cup)

1. Warm the oven in advance at 350 °Fahrenheit. Arrange the tortillas on an ungreased baking sheet. Brush them using a bit of oil and a sprinkle of cheese.
2. Chop and toss the chicken, tomatoes, and seasonings in a large skillet. Simmer and stir using the medium temperature setting (6-8 min.) or until most of the liquid is evaporated.
3. Spoon the delicious mixture over the tortillas.
4. Bake for 15-18 minutes until the tortillas are crisp and cheese is melted. Garnish with the cabbage.

Calories: 206
Carbs: 17 gr.
Protein: 19 gr.
Fat: 6 gr.

Taco Bell's Grilled Steak Soft Tacos

Difficulty ●○○

Cost $ $ $

Servings 6

Preparation Time............ 35 min

Cooking Time................... 15 min

- Large tomatoes (2)
- Red onion (.5 cup)
- Lime juice (.25 cup)
- Jalapeno pepper (1)
- Fresh cilantro (3 tbsp.)
- Salt divided (.75 tsp.)

- Ground cumin divided (2 tsp.)
- Beef flank steak (approx. 1.5 lb.)
- Canola oil (1 tbsp.)
- Whole wheat tortillas (6 warmed8-inches)
- Onion (1 large sliced)
- Optional: Lime wedges & sliced avocado

1. Deseed and chop the tomatoes and jalapeno. Dice the onion and cilantro.
2. Prepare the salsa by combining the first five fixings (before the line). Stir in one teaspoon cumin and 1/4 teaspoon salt. Set it to the side for now.
3. Sprinkle the steak using the rest of the salt and cumin.
4. Grill using the medium temperature setting (with a lid on) until the meat is as you like it (med-rare, on an instant-read thermometer, is about 135 °Fahrenheit), or 6-8 minutes. Let the cooked meat stand for five minutes before slicing.
5. Warm the oil in a skillet using the med-high temperature setting and sauté them until the onion is crisp-tender.
6. Slice steak thinly across the grain and serve on tortillas with onion and salsa.
7. If desired, serve with avocado and lime wedges.

Calories: 329
Protein: 27 gr.
Fat: 12 gr.
Carbs: 29 gr.

Taco Bell's XXL Grilled Stuffed Burrito

Difficulty ●○○

Cost $ $ $

Servings 6

Preparation Time............ 35 min

Cooking Time................... 20 min

- Black beans (.75 cup)
- Whole grain rice medleyex. Santa Fe ready-to-serve (8.5 oz. pkg.)
- 90% Lean ground beef (.5 lb.)
- Frozen corn (.75 cup)
- Salsa of choice (12 oz. jar.) h

- Velvetta thinly sliced processed cheese (4 oz.)
- 10-inch flour tortillas (6warmed)

Optional Toppings:
- Torn lettuce leaves
- Sour cream
- Shredded Mexican cheese blend
- Chopped sweet red pepper & onions
- Also Needed: 4-qt. microwave-safe dish

1. Measure and add the beans into a colander. Thoroughly rinse and drain them.
2. Warm the rice and crumble beef into the baking dish. Thaw and add in the corn and beans.
3. Microwave, covered, using the high-temperature setting until the beef is no longer pink (4-5 min.) and drain.
4. Stir in salsa and cheese and microwave until the cheese is melted (2-3 min.). Fold in rice.
5. Spoon ¾ cup of the beef mixture into the center of each tortilla. Add additional ingredients as desired.
6. Fold the bottom and sides of the tortilla over filling and roll it up. Enjoy them at dinner or anytime!

Calories: 452
Protein: 21 gr.
Fat: 13 gr.
Carbs: 56 gr.

Olive Garden's Eggplant Parmigiana

Difficulty ●●○

Cost $ $ $

Servings 8

Preparation Time............ 1 h

Cooking Time.................... 35 min

- Large eggs (3)
- Panko breadcrumbs (2.5 cups)
- Eggplants (3 medium @ 1/4 inch slices)
- Jars of mushrooms (2 @ 4.5 oz. each)
- Dried basil (.5 tsp.)
- Dried oregano (1/8 tsp.)

- Grated parmesan cheese (.5 cup)
- Part-skim mozzarella cheese (2 cups shredded)
- Spaghetti sauce (28 oz. jar)
- Also 13x9-inch baking dish

1. Drain and slice the mushrooms.
2. Warm the oven to reach 350 °Fahrenheit. Lightly spritz a baking sheet (s) with cooking oil.
3. Place eggs and breadcrumbs into two shallow bowls.
4. Dip the eggplant in the whisked eggs and coat in the crumbs.
5. Arrange them on the prepared trays.
6. Bake for 15-20 minutes, turning once.
7. Drain the mushrooms and mix with the basil and oregano.
8. In another mixing bowl, combine both types of cheese.
9. Spread 1/2 cup of sauce into the prepared baking dish. Layer the fixings using 1/3 portions of each of the mushroom mixture and eggplant, 3/4 cup of sauce, and 1/3 of the cheese mixture. Continue the process in two more layers.
10. Leave the lid off and bake it at 350 °Fahrenheit for 25-30 minutes or until the cheese is melted.

Calories: 305
Protein: 18 gr.
Fat: 12 gr.
Carbs: 32 gr.

Olive Garden's Shrimp & Chicken Carbonara

Difficulty ●●○

Cost $ $ $

Servings 6

Preparation Time............ 1 h

Cooking Time.................. 50 min

- Jumbo shrimp (1 lb.)
- Smoked bacon (8 slices)
- Chicken breast halves (1 lb.)
- Olive oil divided (4 tbsp.)
- Garlic divided (3 tbsp.)
- Italian seasoning (2 tbsp.)

- Linguine pasta (16 oz. pkg.)
- Onion (1)
- Heavy whipping cream (1.5 cups)
- Egg yolks (4)
- Parmesan cheese (1.5 cups grated)
- Freshly cracked black pepper and salt (1 pinch/as desired)
- Sauvignon Blanc wine (.25 cup)

1. Peel and devein the shrimp and dice the bacon. Discard the bones and skin from the chicken. Chop it into bite-sized pieces.
2. Prepare a skillet to warm one tablespoon of oil using the med-high temperature setting. Cook and stir the chicken with one tablespoon of minced garlic and one tablespoon of Italian seasoning (6-8 min.). Dump the chicken into a bowl for now.
3. Warm one tablespoon garlic and one tablespoon olive oil in the same skillet. Fry the shrimp until it's a pinkish-red (6-8 min.). Place it with the chicken.
4. Add water to a large pot and wait for it to boil. Add the rest of the oil (two tablespoons). Cook the linguine until it's al dente (10-12 min.). Dump it into a colander to drain.
5. Toss the bacon into the pan to cook until it's just crispy, not crunchy (6 min.). Drain on two paper towels. Dice and sauté the onion in the bacon grease until translucent (approx. 5 min.).
6. While the onion is sautéing, mix the cream, parmesan cheese, egg yolks, salt, pepper, and rest of the Italian seasoning in a mixing bowl.
7. Measure and add the wine into the pan with the onions. Increase the temperature setting and wait for it to boil. Simmer it until the wine is mostly evaporated (about 2 min.). Add the creamy egg mixture and reduce heat. Simmer until sauce begins to thicken (3-5 min.). Add the chicken and shrimp; mix to coat. Serve on top of a platter of pasta.

Olive Garden's Chicken & Gnocchi Soup

Difficulty ●●○

Cost $ $ $

Servings 8

Preparation Time............ 40 min

Cooking Time.................. 20 min

- Chicken breasts (1 lb.)
- Butter divided (.33 cup)
- Small onion (1)
- Carrot (1 medium)
- Celery (1 rib)
- Coarsely ground pepper (.25 tsp.)

- Garlic (2 cloves)
- All-purpose flour (.33 cup)
- Heavy whipping cream (1.5 cups)
- 2% milk (3.5 cups)
- Chicken bouillon granules (1 tbsp.)
- Potato gnocchi (16 oz. pkg.)
- Fresh spinach (.5 cup)

1. Chop the chicken into 1/2-inch chunks.
2. Brown the chicken in two tablespoons butter using a Dutch oven. Transfer it off the hot burner and keep warm.
3. In the same pan, melt the butter. Chop/mince and toss the onion, carrot, celery, and garlic into the pan to sauté until they are tender.
4. Sift and mix in the flour. Slowly mix in the milk, cream, bouillon, and pepper. Wait for it to boil and adjust the temperature setting to low and cook until thickened (2 min.).
5. Add the gnocchi and spinach. Simmer until the spinach is wilted (3-4 min.). Add the chicken. Cover and simmer until heated thoroughly not boiling for about ten minutes.

Calories: 482
Protein: 21 gr.
Fat: 28 gr.
Carbs: 36 gr.

Olive Garden's Chicken Margherita

Difficulty ●○○

Cost $ $ $

Servings 4

Preparation Time............ 30 min

Cooking Time.................. 30 min

- Whole-wheat spaghetti (8 oz. uncooked)
- Chicken breast halves (4 @ 5 oz. each skinless & boneless)
- Pepper (.5 tsp.)
- Bruschetta topping (1 cup prepared)
- Shredded Italian cheese blend (.33 cup)
- Grated parmesan cheese (2 tbsp.)

1. Warm the oven broiler. Prepare the spaghetti according to the package instructions and drain in a colander.
2. Use a meat mallet to pound the chicken into a 1/2-inch thickness. Sprinkle each piece using pepper.
3. Spritz a skillet with cooking oil spray. Cook the chicken using the medium temperature setting for five to six minutes per side.
4. Transfer the meat to an eight-inch square baking pan. Scoop a portion of the bruschetta topping over the chicken and garnish with the cheeses.
5. Broil it about three to four inches from the burner elements (5-6 min.) or until the cheese is golden brown. Serve with the spaghetti.

Note: Look for the bruschetta topping in your grocer's deli case or the pasta aisle.

Calories: 431
Protein: 40 gr.
Fat: 10 gr.
Carbs: 47 gr.

Olive Garden's Shrimp Fettuccine Alfredo

Difficulty ●○○

Cost $ $ $

Servings 5

Preparation Time............ 25 min

Cooking Time.................. 30 min

- Uncooked fettuccine (12 oz.)
- Olive oil divided (2 tbsp.)
- Jumbo shrimp (1 lb. Uncooked)
- Minced garlic (6 cloves)
- Evaporated milk (12 oz. can)
- Grated parmesan cheese (.25 cup)
- Salt (.5 tsp.)
- Sour cream (.25 cup)
- Drained crabmeat (.5 lb.)
- Fresh basil (.25 cup)

1. Prepare the fettuccine according to package instructions, and set it to the side for now.
2. Peel and devein the shrimp.
3. Warm one tablespoon of oil in a skillet using the med-high temperature setting.
4. Add the shrimp and simmer until they have turned pink (4 min.). Transfer the batch to a holding container to keep warm for now.
5. Heat the same pan (medium temp) to warm the rest of the oil.
6. Mince and toss in the garlic to sauté for one to two minutes. Mix in the milk and salt and wait for it to boil, continually stirring.
7. Transfer the pan to a cool burner and fold in cheese until melted. Whisk in the sour cream.
8. Combine the mixture with the fettuccine and add the shrimp and crab.
9. Warm and stir in the basil to serve.

Calories: 538
Protein: 40 gr.
Fat: 16 gr.
Carbs: 56 gr.

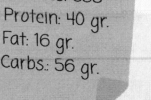

Chick-fil-A's Chicken Biscuit

Difficulty ● ● ●

Cost $ $ $

Servings 4

Preparation Time............ 60 min

Cooking Time.................. 50 min

- A-P flour (1.25 cups)
- Salt (.5 tsp.)
- Baking powder (1 tbsp.)
- Chilled unsalted butter (.25 cup)
- Cold buttermilk (.5 cup)
- Honey (.5 tbsp.)
- The Chicken:
- Dill pickle juice (.33 cup)
- Milk (2/3 cup)

- Boneless chicken breast (1 lb.)
- Eggs (2)
- Breadcrumbs (.75 cup)
- Powdered sugar (2 tbsp.)
- All-Pur. flour (.75 cup)
- Kosher salt (2 tsp.)
- Chili powder (.25 tsp.)
- Black pepper (.5 tsp.)
- Peanut oil

1. Prepare the Biscuits: Preheat the oven at 425° Fahrenheit.
2. Measure and add the salt, flour, and baking powder in a food processor, pulsing to mix.
3. Cube and add the butter to create coarse crumbs, dumping it into a mixing container. Scoop a hole in the center to add the honey and buttermilk. Do not overwork it, stirring with a spatula until just combined.
4. Lightly flour a cutting board. Scoop the dough onto the board, rolling it until it is about one inch thick. Knead the dough to process six times.
5. Gently roll the dough into a rectangular shape until it's about 1/2-inch thick.
6. Use a three-inch biscuit cutter to make eight biscuits. Scoop the scraps to make another biscuit.
7. Add a layer of parchment baking paper over a baking sheet. Gently brush each biscuit with buttermilk. Set a timer to bake until the tops are golden (15 min.). Transfer to the top of the stovetop and brush with melted butter.
8. Prepare the Chicken: Pound the chicken breasts into a 1/2-inch thickness and cut in half. Put them into a zipper-type bag with the whisked eggs, milk, and pickle juice. Marinate the chicken in the fridge for about half an hour.
9. Toss the breadcrumbs into the food processor and pulse until they're finely crushed. Toss and whisk the salt, flour, breadcrumbs, sugar, black pepper, and chili powder in a mixing bowl.
10. Dip the breasts of chicken in the mixture and wait for about five minutes before cooking them.
11. Add oil to a cast-iron skillet (1/2-inch deep) using the medium temperature setting. Cook the chicken in batches if needed for about two to three minutes per side.
12. Slice the freshly made biscuit and serve promptly.

Chick-fil-A's Chicken Egg & Cheese Biscuit

Difficulty ●○○

Cost $ $ $

Servings 5

Preparation Time............ 25 min

Cooking Time................... 30 min

- Pickle juice (.5 cup)
- Whole milk (.5 cup)
- Garlic & onion powder (.5 tsp. each)
- Chicken thighs (2.5 lb.)
- Egg (1)
- Dry Mixture For The Chicken:
- A-P flour (3 cups)
- Baking powder (2 tbsp.)
- Kosher salt (1 tbsp.)
- Powdered sugar (.25 cup)

- Paprika (1 tbsp.)
- Chili powder (2 tsp.)
- Refrigerated buttermilk biscuits (6 oz.)
- Cheesy Eggs:
- Cooking oil spray (as needed)
- Milk (.25 cup)
- Large eggs (8)
- Kosher salt (2 tsp.)
- Cheddar cheese (5 slices)

1. Warm the oven according to directions on the package of biscuits.
2. Attach a deep-frying thermometer to the side of a large heavy-bottomed pot or Dutch oven. Warm about 2.5 inches of oil using the medium temperature setting (325° Fahrenheit). Cover a baking tray using a few paper towels.
3. Whisk the wet fixings in a medium bowl. Place the chicken into marinade.
4. As the oil heats, whisk the dry ingredients.
5. Reserving the marinade, transfer the chicken to a bowl.
6. Whisk the egg into the marinade. Dip the chicken into the egg mixture, one piece at a time, shaking off excess egg mixture. Dredge chicken pieces in the flour mix, making sure to coat evenly on both sides.
7. Repeat the breading process (egg mixture to flour mixture) one more time, and set chicken aside.
8. Once the oil is heated, cook the chicken for about two to three minutes on each side until well done.
9. As the chicken cooks, prepare the biscuits according to package directions. Place cooked chicken on the prepared baking sheet to drain. Set biscuits aside.
10. Scramble the Eggs: Reset the oven temperature at 350° Fahrenheit. Generously spray a small rimmed baking sheet (9x13) with cooking oil spray. In a medium bowl, reserving the sliced cheddar cheese, whisk the folded egg fixings until pale in color and frothy.
11. Dump the egg mixture into the baking sheet. Cook until the mixture is slightly wobbly, but set in the center, about six to eight minutes, rotating the pan halfway through.
12. Cover the baking tray with a cutting board for about four minutes, or until the egg is set in center, but still tender.
13. With two hands, use kitchen towels to the sandwich baking sheet and cutting board. Flip the "sandwich" over, placing the board on the kitchen counter.
14. Lift the pan and slice the cooked egg crosswise into five even strips. Gently fold each slice in half lengthwise and transfer, using a thin spatula, back onto the baking tray. Top with cheese to bake for two to three minutes, or until the cheese is melted.
15. Split each biscuit in half and top each with chicken, egg, and remaining biscuit top. Serve immediately.

Chick-fil-A's Sandwich

Difficulty ●○○

Cost $ $$

Servings 4

Preparation Time............ 60 min

Cooking Time................... 50 min

- Hamburger buns (4split)
- Lettuce (1 head)
- Dill pickle (20 slices)
- Sliced tomato (1)
- Chicken breasts (2)
- Milk divided (1.5 cups)
- Dill pickle juice (1 cup)

- Egg (1 large)
- All-purpose flour (.5 cup)
- Kosher salt and freshly cracked black pepper (as desired)
- Confectioners' sugar (1 tbsp.)
- Peanut oil (1 cup)

1. Slice the breast of chicken in half horizontally on a cutting board, trimming away the fat.
2. Whisk the pickle juice and 1/2 cup milk. Toss in the chicken and marinate it for about 30 minutes. Drain well.
3. Prepare a skillet using the medium-temperature setting to warm the oil.
4. Prepare another container and whisk egg and last cup of milk. Fold in the chicken to coat.
5. In a gallon-sized zipper-type bag, combine the flour, salt, pepper, and confectioners' sugar. Toss in the chicken and shake to cover.
6. Arrange the chicken in the skillet and fry for four to five minutes. (Prepare in batches if needed and drain on paper towels.)
7. Serve the chicken promptly on buns with lettuce, pickles, and tomatoes.

Calories: 454.6
Carbs: 44.2 gr.
Protein: 28.6 gr.
Fat: 18.2 gr.

Chick-fil-A's Market Salad

Difficulty ● ○ ○

Cost $ $ $

Servings 4

Preparation Time............ 25 min

Cooking Time.................. 10 min

- Chicken breast (2)
- Olive oil (1 tbsp.)
- Coarse black pepper (1/8 tsp.)
- Kosher salt (.25 tsp.)
- Paprika (.25 tsp.)
- Cayenne pepper (1/8 tsp.)
- Chopped spring salad mix (16 cups)
- Blueberries (1 cup)
- Chopped Granny Smith apple (1)
- Strawberries (1 cup halved)
- Salt (1 tsp.)

- Crumbled blue cheese (.5 cup)
- Granola (1 cup)
- Roasted walnuts (1 cup)
- Zesty apple cider vinaigrette (1 cup below)
- Olive oil (.66 cup)
- Lime juice (3 tbsp.)
- Honey (.25 cup)
- Apple cider vinegar (.25 cup)
- Black pepper (.5 tsp.)
- Garlic powder (.5 tsp.)

1. Combine the oil, chicken, cayenne, black pepper, salt, and pepper.
2. Warm a skillet using the medium temperature setting. Cook the chicken for five to eight minutes per side. Cool the chicken and prepare the salad.
3. Prepare the vinaigrette using the listed fixings and shake it thoroughly before using it.
4. Layer the lettuce, cabbage, carrots, strawberries, blueberries, apple, walnuts, granola, and blue cheese. Thinly slice and add the chicken.
5. Spritz with the chilled dressing and serve.

Calories: 311
Protein: 30 gr.
Fat: 12 gr.
Carbs: 22 gr.

Chick-fil-A's Sweet Carrot Salad

Difficulty ●○○

Cost $ $ $

Servings 8

Preparation Time............ 40 min

Cooking Time................... /

- Grated carrots (1 lb.)
- Raisins (.5 cup)
- Crushed pineapple (1 cup)
- Lemon juice (1 dash)
- Honey (1 tbsp.)
- Mayonnaise (2 tbsp.)

1. Chop/mince the carrots, pineapple, and raisins.

2. Mix in the honey, lemon juice, and mayo.

3. Pop it in the fridge for at least half an hour before serving.

Calories: 105
Protein: 1 gr.
Fat: 2.9 gr.
Carbs: 20.6 gr.

Chick-fil-A's Chick Nuggets

Difficulty ●○○

Cost $ $ $

Servings 4

Preparation Time............ 40 min

Cooking Time................... 25 min

- Large eggs (2)
- Milk (1 cup)
- Chicken breast (1-inch cubes1 lb.)
- Flour (.75 cup)
- Breadcrumbs (.75 cup)
- Powdered sugar (2 tbsp.)

- White pepper (.5 tsp.)
- Kosher salt (2 tsp.)
- Chili powder (.25 tsp.)
- Peanut oil (3-inches in the skillet)

1. Toss the breadcrumbs into a food processor, pulsing until they're fine.
2. Use a zipper-type baggie and add the pieces of chicken, whisked, eggs, and milk.
3. Place the marinated chicken in the fridge for about 15-20 minutes.
4. Pour three inches of oil into a Dutch oven and heat using the med-high temperature setting.
5. Measure and whisk the powdered sugar, flour, breadcrumbs, salt, white pepper, and chili powder into a shallow dish.
6. Dip the chicken into the flour mix. Wait a minute and fry in batches (2-3 min.). Transfer them onto a baking tray to serve promptly. Don't use towels to drain because it could soften/steam the nuggets.

Calories: 379
Protein: 33 gr.
Fat: 8 gr.
Carbs: 39 gr.

Chick-fil-A's Honey Mustard Grilled Chicken

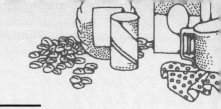

Difficulty ●○○

Cost $ $ $

Servings 4

Preparation Time............ 35 min

Cooking Time.................. 20 min

- Dijon mustard (.33 cup)
- Honey (.25 cup)
- Mayonnaise (2 tbsp.)
- Steak sauce (1 tsp.)
- Chicken breast halves (4no skin or bones)

1. Lightly oil the grate and warm the grill using the medium temperature setting.
2. Prepare a shallow dish with the steak sauce, mayo, honey, and mustard. Set aside a portion for basting and rest for the coating sauce.
3. Grill the chicken for about 20 minutes, turning intermittently.
4. Baste using the reserved sauce the last ten minutes of the cooking cycle.

Calories: 265.9
Protein: 24.7 gr.
Fat: 8.3 gr.
Carbs: 22 gr.

Sweet

Applebee's Triple Chocolate Meltdown

Difficulty ● ○ ○

Cost $ $ $

Servings 4

Preparation Time............ 35 min

Cooking Time.................. 20 min

- 4 ounces semisweet chocolate chips
- 1/2 cup (1 stick) butter, plus more for greasing
- 2 large whole eggs
- 2 large egg yolks
- 1/4 cup sugar, plus more for dusting
- 2 tablespoons all-purpose flour
- 1/4 teaspoon salt

- Toppings
- 4 ounces white chocolate
- 4 ounces semisweet chocolate
- 2 teaspoons vegetable shortening, divided
- 4 scoops vanilla ice cream

1. Preheat oven to 400°F. Grease muffin pans or ramekins and dust with sugar. Melt chocolate chips with butter over a double boiler, whisking until smooth.
2. In a separate bowl, whisk together the whole eggs, yolks, and sugar until light and fluffy.
3. Whisk both mixtures together.
4. Gradually add flour and salt, whisking until blended.
5. Distribute evenly into prepared pans and arrange on a baking sheet.
6. Bake until edges are done and centers are still soft (about 8 minutes).
7. Invert onto dessert plate.
8. Prepare toppings. Place each type of chocolate in separate, microwave-safe bowls. Add a teaspoon of shortening to each bowl. Microwave for about 15 seconds and stir. Repeat until smooth.
9. Top the cake pieces with ice cream and drizzle with melted chocolate.

Calories 727,
Total Fat 31 gr.
Carbs 107 gr.
Protein 11 gr.

BJ's Pizookie

Difficulty ●○○

Cost $ $ $

Servings 4

Preparation Time............ 10 min

Cooking Time.................. 10 min

- Nonstick cooking spray
- 1 1/8 cups all-purpose flour
- 1/4 teaspoon baking soda
- 1/2 teaspoon salt
- 1/2 cup (1 stick) butter or shortening
- 1/4 cup brown sugar

- 1/2 cup granulated sugar
- 1 large egg, beaten
- 1 teaspoon vanilla
- 1 cup chocolate chips or chunks
- 2-3 scoops of vanilla ice cream, or any flavor choice

1. Preheat oven to 350°F. Grease a 9-inch round pan.

2. Sift first 3 ingredients together in a bowl and set aside.

3. Cream the butter and sugars.

4. Add egg and vanilla, then beat until fluffy.

5. Add sifted dry ingredients and mix just to incorporate.

6. Stir in chocolate chips.

7. Spread dough evenly in pan.

8. Bake until edges are slightly browned and begin to separate from pan (about 10 minutes).

9. Serve with ice cream.

Calories 222,
Total Fat 11.8 gr.
Carbs 26.1 gr.
Protein 2.8 gr

KFC's Chocolate Chip Cake

Difficulty ●○○

Cost $ $ $

Servings 10

Preparation Time............ 10 min

Cooking Time.................. 45 min

- 1 (151/4-ounce) box devil's food cake mix
- 1 (3.4-ounce) package instant chocolate pudding
- 1 cup sour cream
- 4 eggs, beaten
- 1/2 cup water

- 1/2 cup canola oil
- 1 1/2 cups chocolate chips
- Cream Cheese Frosting
- 1/4 cup unsalted butter, softened
- 4 ounces cream cheese, softened
- 3 cups powdered sugar
- 1 tablespoon milk

1. Preheat oven to 350°F. Grease and flour a Bundt cake pan.
2. In a large bowl, mix cake and pudding mixes together.
3. Use an electric mixer at slow speed and add sour cream, eggs, water, and oil until blended.
4. Drop in chocolate chips and mix briefly to distribute.
5. Transfer to Bundt pan.
6. Bake until toothpick inserted near the center comes out clean (about 45-50 minutes).
7. Leave in pan to cool for 20 minutes.
8. Remove from pan and place on a wire rack.
9. Prepare the frosting. Use a mixer to beat butter and cream cheese together until fluffy. Add the rest of the ingredients for frosting and beat 3-5 minutes longer. If too thick, add more milk drop by drop until the right consistency is achieved.
10. Pipe or drizzle the frosting over the top of the cooled cake. Let the frosting flow down the edges of the cake.

Calories 300,
Total Fat 12 gr.
Carbs 49 gr.
Protein 3 gr.

Longhorn Chocolate Stampede

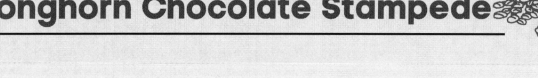

Difficulty ●●●

Cost $ $ $

Servings 12

Preparation Time............ 8 h

Cooking Time.................. 1 h

Brownie Base
- 1 box fudge brownie mix, plus required ingredients*
- Cake Layer
- 1 box devil's food cake mix, plus required ingredients*

Mousse
- 3 ounces semisweet chocolate, coarsely chopped
- 3 ounces milk chocolate, coarsely chopped
- 2 cups heavy whipping cream, very cold
- 2 tablespoons powdered sugar

Ganache
- 1 1/2 cups heavy whipping cream
- 2 tablespoons unsalted butter
- 18 ounces semisweet chocolate, chopped
- Accompaniments
- Whipped cream
- Vanilla ice cream
- Chocolate syrup
- * Use espresso or strong coffee when water is called for.

1. Prepare the fudge brownie and devil's food cake according to packaging instructions. Replace water for strong coffee or espresso. Use the same pan size for both. After baking, cool slightly, then remove from pans and place on wire rack to cool further. Both must be completely cooled before adding the mousse layer.
2. Prepare the mousse. Melt the chocolate in the microwave or double boiler. Using an electric mixer with the whisk attachment, whip the cold cream and sugar until stiff peaks form. Fold one-third of the whipped cream into the melted chocolate. Add this to the remaining whipped cream and fold gently until uniform in color.
3. Spread the mousse evenly over the brownie base. Top with the devil's food cake layer. Cover with plastic wrap and refrigerate for 1 hour to overnight.
4. Prepare the ganache. In a heat-safe bowl, place the chocolate and butter. Place the cream in a separate heat-safe bowl and bring to a boil over a double boiler or using the microwave. For the microwave, heat for 1 minute and whisk the cream. Heat again 10 seconds at a time until bubbling starts. Remove immediately from microwave. For double boiler, whisk continuously and remove from heat as soon as bubbling starts. Pour the boiling cream into the chocolate-butter mixture and let stand for 2 minutes. Let cool down to room temperature.
5. Spread the cooled ganache over the chilled layered cake-with-mousse.
6. Chill the whole cake for at least 6 hours to overnight.
7. Warm the knife first (you may dip it in hot water) and cut into 12 wedges.
8. Add dollops of whipped cream and scoops of ice cream.
9. Drizzle with chocolate syrup and serve.

Olive Garden's Lemon Cream Cake

Difficulty ●○○

Cost $ $ $

Servings 10

Preparation Time............ 45 min

Cooking Time.................... 60 min

Cake
- 1 cup cake flour
- 1 1/4 cups sugar, divided
- 1 cup egg whites (about 8 egg whites)
- 1 teaspoon cream of tartar
- 1/2 teaspoon salt
- 1 teaspoon vanilla
- 2 tablespoons powdered sugar, for dusting

Crumb Topping (optional)
- 2 cups all-purpose flour
- 5 teaspoons granulated sugar
- 1/2 teaspoon salt
- 1/2 cup (1 stick) butter, melted
- 1 teaspoon lemon juice
- 3 teaspoons water

Lemon Cream Filling
- 1 cup heavy cream
- 1 (8-ounce) package cream cheese
- 2 1/2 cups powdered sugar
- 3 tablespoons lemon juice

1. Preheat oven to 350°F.
2. Prepare the cake. Combine the flour and 1/4 cup sugar and sift 4 times. To a grease-free mixing bowl, add egg whites, cream of tartar and salt. Using a whisk attachment, beat until frothy. While beating, add the remaining sugar gradually until mixture is fine-textured, with soft peaks. Add vanilla and fold in flour mixture, about 1/4 cup at a time. Pour evenly into an ungreased 9-inch tube pan. Run a spatula through the batter to break up large air bubbles. Bake until toothpick inserted at center comes out clean (about 45-60 minutes). Invert to pan and let cool completely. Use a serrated knife to cut into 2 or 3 layers. Keep chilled until ready to be assembled.
3. Crumb topping (if using): Preheat oven to 350°F and line a baking sheet. In a mixer bowl, combine the flour, sugar and salt. Beat to blend. Add the melted butter, lemon juice and water and beat until well-blended. Add more water by the teaspoon if the mixture looks like sand. The mixture should form pea-sized clusters. Keep the sizes uniform for even baking and texture. Spread in an even layer on baking sheet and bake until golden brown (about 15 minutes). Let cool. If cooked clusters are too large and hard to break with the back of a spoon, use a blender or food processor.
4. Cream Filling: In an electric mixer, whip the cream until soft peaks form. In another bowl, beat the cream cheese, sugar and lemon juice until smooth. Gently fold into the whipped cream until well-blended. Refrigerate for at least 30 minutes.
5. To assemble the cake.
6. Frost bottom layer with filling (1/2 of mixture for 2 layers or 1/3 for 3 layers).
7. Repeat for second layer (if using 3 layers).
8. Top with the last cake layer. Keep chilled.
9. Just before serving, dust with powdered sugar and sprinkle with crumb topping (optional).

Magnolia Bakery's Vanilla Cupcakes

Difficulty ●○○

Cost $ $ $

Servings 24

Preparation Time............ 20 min

Cooking Time................... 25 min

- 1 1/2 cups self-rising flour
- 1 1/4 cups cake flour
- 2 cups granulated sugar
- 1 cup unsalted butter, at room temperature, cubed
- 1 cup whole milk
- 1 teaspoon pure vanilla extract
- 4 large eggs, at room temperature, lightly beaten

- Frosting
- 1 cup (2 sticks) unsalted butter, at room temperature
- 1 teaspoon vanilla extract
- 4 cups powdered sugar
- 2 tablespoons whole milk, + 1 tablespoon more if needed
- Food coloring of choice, if desired
- Sprinkles, candy to decorate, if desired

1. Preheat oven to 350°F. Line cupcake pans with paper liners.
2. In a large bowl, combine the self-rising flour, cake flour, and sugar. Use an electric mixer with paddle attachment and mix at low speed to blend.
3. Add butter, one cube at a time, until batter looks coarse.
4. Stir vanilla into milk and add to batter alternately with eggs, still at slow speed. Scrape down sides of bowl as needed.
5. Fill the cupcake pans about ¾ full.
6. Bake until toothpick inserted at center comes out clean (about 20-25 minutes).
7. Place on wire rack and allow to cool completely.
8. Prepare frosting. Cream the butter and add vanilla. Keep mixing while adding sugar a cup at a time. Add milk and mix until creamy. If too thick, add more milk, a drop at a time. If desired, add a few drops of food color and mix. Use a spatula or piping bag to frost the cupcakes.
9. Decorate, if desired

Calories 400,
Total Fat 16 gr.
Carbs 28 gr.
Protein 3 gr.

Cheesecake Factory's Key Lime Pie Cheesecake

Difficulty ● ○ ○

Cost $ $ $

Servings 10

Preparation Time............ 20 min

Cooking Time................... 15 min

Crust
- 5 tablespoons butter, melted
- 2 tablespoons sugar
- 1 cup graham cracker crumbs

Filling
- 1 envelope unflavored gelatin
- ¾ cup key lime juice
- 1 1/4 cups sugar
- 4 eggs, at room temperature
- 2 egg yolks, at room temperature
- 2 tablespoons grated key lime zest

1 pound cream cheese, at room temperature

- 2 egg whites, at room temperature
- 1/8 teaspoon salt
- 1/4 cup sugar
- Candied zest
- 1 cup water
- 1 cup sugar
- Rind of 2 limes, julienned
- Topping (optional)
- Whipped cream
- Lime zest

1. Mix crust ingredients together well. Spread and press into a lined spring form pan. Cover and place in refrigerator to chill.
2. Place gelatin in a saucepan with key lime juice and stir until dissolved (about 5 minutes).
3. Whisk in sugar, eggs, egg yolks and zest.
4. Cook on medium heat, whisking frequently, until very thick (about 10 minutes).
5. Remove from heat and let cool slightly.
6. Meanwhile, beat the cream cheese using an electric mixer until smooth.
7. Keep mixing at medium speed while gradually adding the lime mixture until well-blended and smooth.
8. Let cool completely.
9. Transfer to a bowl and cover.
10. Place in refrigerator to cool, stirring every 10 to 15 minutes until fully chilled.
11. Using a whisk attachment, beat the egg whites, salt and sugar to form stiff (but not dry) peaks.
12. Gently fold egg whites into chilled lime mixture until well-blended.
13. Pour over crust in spring form pan, spreading evenly with a spatula.
14. Cover with plastic wrap, making sure it touches the surface, to prevent a film from forming.
15. Let chill to set (at least 4 hours).
16. Prepare candied zest. Combine water and sugar in a saucepan and heat over medium heat. Stir until sugar is dissolved. Add lime zest and let simmer for 3 minutes. Remove zest and let dry over parchment paper. Chill while drying.
17. Remove chilled cheesecake from pan.
18. Garnish with whipped cream (optional) and candied zest.

California Pizza Kitchen's Pumpkin Cheesecake

Difficulty ●○○

Cost $ $

Servings 8

Preparation Time............ 15 min

Cooking Time.................... 1 h

Crust
- 1 1/2 cups graham cracker crumbs
- 1/4 cup sugar
- 6 tablespoons unsalted butter, melted
- 1/2 teaspoon cinnamon
- 1/2 teaspoon ground ginger

Cheesecake
- 1/3 cup all-purpose flour

1 1/2 teaspoons ground cinnamon

- 1/8 teaspoon each ground cardamom, ground cloves, ground ginger and ground nutmeg
- 3 (8-ounce) packages cream cheese
- 1 1/2 cups dark brown sugar, packed
- 1 1/8 cups sour cream
- 3 large eggs
- 2 teaspoons vanilla extract
- 1 1/4 cups canned pumpkin puree
- Whipped cream, for garnish

1. Prepare the crust by combining the ingredients until well-blended. You may use a blender or food processor for a finer crust. Press evenly and well into a lined spring form pan.
2. Preheat the oven to 350°F.
3. For the cheesecake, combine the first 3 (dry) ingredients well and set aside.
4. Using an electric mixer, beat the cream cheese until softened.
5. Add sugar and continue beating, scraping sides when needed, until creamy and well-incorporated.
6. Add the flour mixture and beat until well-blended.
7. Beat in sour cream.
8. Drop eggs in one at a time, beating well and scraping down after each addition.
9. Lastly, add the vanilla and pumpkin puree and beat until well-blended.
10. Pour mixture into pan with crust.
11. Bake until center is firm (about 1 hour) or until internal temperature is 180°F.
12. Place on a wire rack to cool.
13. Refrigerate overnight to set.
14. Remove from pan and serve with whipped cream.

Cheesecake Factory's Caramel Pecan Turtle Cheesecake

Difficulty ● ● ●

Cost $ $ $

Servings 8

Preparation Time............ 20 min

Cooking Time................... 50 min

Brownie Crust
- 2/3 Cup butter, melted
- 1 1/4 cups sugar
- ¾ cup cocoa powder
- 2 eggs
- 1 teaspoon vanilla extract
- 1/2 cup all-purpose flour

1/2 cup pecans, chopped

Cheesecake
- 1 (16-ounce) pack cream cheese
- 1/3 Cup sugar
- 1/4 cup sour cream
- 2 large eggs
- 1 teaspoon vanilla

Toppings
- 1/4 cup caramel sauce, plus more for drizzling
- 1/4 cup chocolate sauce, plus more for drizzling
- 1/2 cup chopped pecans

1. Preheat oven to 325°F. Line and butter a spring form pan.
2. Whisk sugar and cocoa into melted butter.
3. While continuously whisking, add eggs and vanilla.
4. Stir in flour, just to incorporate.
5. Add pecans and stir briefly.
6. Pour into prepared pan and spread evenly with a spatula.
7. Bake until fragrant and edges begin to pull away from pan (about 15 minutes).
8. While crust is baking, mix filling ingredients in a bowl until smooth.
9. Pour filling over crust and spread evenly with a spatula.
10. In a small bowl or cup, mix caramel and chocolate sauces together.
11. Pour sauce over filling.
12. Bake until center is firm (about 35 minutes).
13. Drizzle with more caramel-and-chocolate sauce.
14. Sprinkle with pecans.
15. May be served hot or cold.

Calories 820,
Total Fat 61 gr.
Carbs 75 gr.
Protein 13 gr.

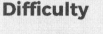

Cheesecake Factory's White Chocolate Raspberry Truffle Cheesecake

Difficulty ● ○ ○

Cost $ $ $

Servings 8

Preparation Time............ 2 h + overnight refrigeration

Cooking Time.................. 75 min

- Oreo Crust
- 1 1/2 cups Oreo baking crumbs
- 1/3 cup butter, melted
- Raspberry Sauce
- 10 ounces fresh raspberries, washed, rinsed and dried with paper towels
- 1/4 cup sugar
- 2 tablespoons lemon juice
- Filling
- 4 (8-ounce) packs cream cheese, at room temperature

- F1 1/4 cups sugar
- 1/2 cup sour cream, at room temperature
- 2 teaspoons vanilla
- 5 eggs, at room temperature
- 4 ounces white chocolate, chopped

Garnish

- 1 cup heavy whipping cream
- 1/2 cup powdered sugar
- White chocolate shavings, for garnish

1. Preheat oven to 475°F. Line a spring form pan. Wrap the outer part of the pan with aluminum foil as well.
2. Place a large pan filled 1/2-inch deep with water in the oven as it heats. Make sure to maintain the water at this level.
3. Combine the crumbs and butter well and press into the bottom of the spring form pan. Cover and freeze until filling is ready.
4. To make the raspberry sauce, combine the ingredients in a saucepan and bring to a boil. With constant stirring, simmer until raspberries are broken down. Strain into a mixing bowl and let cool. Set aside.
5. Place cream cheese, sugar, sour cream and vanilla in a bowl for an electric mixer. Set speed to low and mix until smooth.
6. Add eggs one at a time, while mixing, until well-blended.
7. Sprinkle the bottom of the crust with the chopped white chocolate.
8. Pour half of the filling into the pan, spreading with a spatula.
9. Scoop out about 1/3 cup of the cooled raspberry sauce and store any remaining sauce for future recipes.
10. Pour half of the scooped raspberry sauce into the filling and then make a quick swirl with a butter knife.
11. Add the rest of the filling and swirl in the remaining raspberry sauce.
12. Place the pan (with outer bottom lined) in the water bath.
13. Bake for 12 minutes, then reduce oven temperature to 350°F.
14. Continue baking until top of cheesecake turns light brown (about 1 hour).
15. Do not open the oven. Leave the pan in the oven to cool completely (about 1-2 hours).
16. Remove from oven, cover with plastic wrap and refrigerate overnight.
17. Whip the cream and powdered sugar rapidly (about 5 minutes).
18. Remove cheesecake from pan and sprinkle with white chocolate shavings.
19. Serve with whipped cream.

Buca Di Beppo's Italian Crème Cake

Difficulty ●○○

Cost $ $ $

Servings 8-12

Preparation Time............ 40 min

Cooking Time.................. 30 min

Cake

- 2 cups all-purpose flour
- 2 teaspoons baking powder
- 1/2 teaspoon salt
- Juice and zest of 1 medium lemon
- 1/2 cup unsalted butter, softened
- 1 1/4 cups granulated sugar
- 3 large eggs
- 1 cup milk

Filling and Frosting

- 8 ounces mascarpone, softened
- 1 cup heavy cream, plus more for garnish (if desired)
- 1/2 cup lemon curd
- Raspberry Sauce
- 12 ounces fresh raspberries
- 1 tablespoon sugar
- 1 tablespoon brandy (optional)

1. Preheat oven to 350°F. Line and butter two 9-inch round pans.
2. In a bowl, combine flour, baking powder, salt, and lemon zest, then set aside.
3. Using an electric mixer, cream the butter and sugar until light and fluffy.
4. Keeping speed at medium, add eggs one at a time, mixing well after each addition.
5. Mix in the lemon juice and reduce speed to low.
6. Add dry ingredients and milk alternately until well-blended.
7. Pour equal amounts into prepared pans and spread evenly.
8. Bake until a toothpick inserted into the center of the cakes comes out clean (about 30 minutes).
9. Cool the cakes in the pans for 10 minutes.
10. Remove from pans and let cool completely on a wire rack.
11. While the cakes are cooling, prepare the frosting/filling. Mix the ingredients until smooth. If needed, cover with plastic wrap and keep refrigerated while waiting for cakes to cool completely.
12. To prepare the raspberry sauce, mix the ingredients using a food processor or blender. Cover and refrigerate until ready to use.
13. If needed, slice off any uneven parts of the tops of the cakes. Spread with frosting and place one on top of the other.
14. Pipe whipped cream over frosting, if desired, and drizzle with raspberry sauce.

Buca Di Beppo's Tiramisu

Difficulty ● ● ●

Cost $ $ $

Servings 1-2

Preparation Time............ 10 min

Cooking Time.................../

- 3 pieces 6-inch round savoiardi (or an equivalent amount of ladyfingers to make 3 layers)
- 1/2 cup espresso rum mix
- 3 ounces zabaglione custard
- 9 ounces sweet mascarpone
- 1/2 ounce cocoa powder
- 1/8 cup biscotti, crumbled

1. Dip one round savoiardi in espresso rum mix and place in serving bowl (about 3 inches deep and 7 inches wide).
2. Spread with a third of the zabaglione, then a third of the mascarpone.
3. Repeat with the rest of the dipped biscuits, zabaglione and mascarpone, to make 3 layers.
4. Chill before serving.
5. Sprinkle with cocoa powder and crumbled biscotti.
6. Serve.

Calories 267,
Total Fat 6 gr.
Carbs 29 gr.
Protein 6 gr.

Starbucks' Iced Lemon Pound Cake

Difficulty ● ○ ○

Cost $ $ $

Servings 8

Preparation Time............ 10 min

Cooking Time.................. 50 min

Loaf
- 1 1/2 cups all-purpose flour
- 2 teaspoons baking powder
- 1/2 teaspoon salt
- 3 large eggs
- 1 cup granulated sugar
- 1 cup sour cream

- 1/2 cup vegetable oil
- 2 tablespoons lemon zest
- 1 tablespoon lemon extract, or to taste

Lemon Glaze
- 1 cup powdered sugar
- 3 tablespoons lemon juice

1. Preheat oven to 350°F. Grease and flour a loaf pan.
2. In a bowl, combine flour, baking powder and salt. Set aside.
3. In a mixer bowl, beat the eggs, sugar, and sour cream until well-blended.
4. Continue beating while adding oil in a stream.
5. Add lemon zest and extract and mix.
6. Add the flour mixture and mix just to incorporate. The batter will be lumpy.
7. Pour batter into prepared loaf pan and spread evenly with a spatula.
8. Bake for 40 minutes and then tent with foil.
9. Let bake until toothpick inserted at the center comes out with just a few crumbs (about 10-12 minutes).
10. Place pan on a wire rack for loaf to cool completely.
11. Meanwhile, prepare the glaze. Whisk powdered sugar while adding lemon juice gradually until the right consistency is achieved.
12. Remove loaf from pan and drizzle with glaze.

Calories 428,
Total Fat 18 gr.
Carbs 63 gr.
Protein 5 gr.

Corner Bakery Café's Cinnamon Crème Coffee Cake

Difficulty ● ○ ○

Cost $ $ $

Servings 8-12

Preparation Time............ 30 min

Cooking Time................... 75 min

Filling and Streusel
- 1/2 cup sugar
- 2/3 Cup brown sugar
- 1 tablespoon cinnamon
- 1/4 teaspoon nutmeg
- 22/3 cups flour
- 1 cup (2 sticks) butter, melted

Cake
- 3 cups flour
- 2 teaspoons baking powder
- 1 teaspoon baking soda
- 1/4 teaspoon salt
- 1/2 cup (1 stick) butter, diced, at room temperature
- 1/2 cup vegetable shortening
- 1 1/2 cups sugar
- 5 eggs
- 1 1/2 teaspoons vanilla
- 2 cups sour cream
- Powdered sugar, for dusting

1. Preheat oven to 350°F. Grease and flour a tube pan.
2. First prepare the streusel. In a bowl, mix together sugars, cinnamon, nutmeg and flour.
3. Add the melted butter and mix to form large morsels (do not break into fine crumbs).
4. Now prepare the cake batter. Combine flour, baking powder, baking soda and salt. Set aside.
5. In a large bowl, place the butter and shortening.
6. Add sugar and beat until light and creamy.
7. Beat in vanilla.
8. Gradually add the flour mixture and sour cream, alternately, to make a thick batter.
9. Put half of the batter into the tube pan and put half of the streusel over it.
10. Add the remaining batter and top with the remaining streusel, gently pressing down to set into the batter.
11. Bake until toothpick inserted near center comes out clean (about 1 hour 15 minutes).
12. Let cool for 30 minutes.
13. Remove from pan and let cool on a wire rack.
14. Dust with powdered sugar.

Calories 780,
Total Fat 37 gr.
Carbs 104 gr.
Protein 0.8 gr.

Starbucks' Raspberry Swirl Pound Cake

Difficulty ● ○ ○

Cost $ $ $

Servings 8

Preparation Time............ 30 min

Cooking Time................... 60 min

- 1 box pound cake mix
- 1/4 cup (1/2 stick) butter, at room temperature
- 2 eggs
- 2/3 cup milk
- 1 teaspoon lemon juice
- 1/3 cup raspberry spread
- 6 drops red food color (optional)

- Cream Cheese Frosting
- 1 (8-ounce) package cream cheese, at room temperature
- 1 cup powdered sugar
- 1 teaspoon lemon juice

1. Preheat oven to 350°F. Grease and flour a loaf pan.
2. Mix cake mix, milk, butter and eggs with an electric mixer, at low speed, until blended (about 30 seconds). Switch speed to medium and mix 2 minutes more.
3. Pour about 1/3 of the batter into a separate bowl, for the raspberry swirl.
4. To the original bowl, mix in lemon juice.
5. To the other bowl, mix in raspberry spread and food color (if using).
6. Pour about 1/2 of the white batter into the loaf pan.
7. Pour about 1/2 of the raspberry batter on top.
8. Repeat layering red and white layers.
9. Cut through the batter with a spatula, lengthwise, to create the swirl.
10. Bake until just a few crumbs stick to a toothpick inserted at the center (about 55-60 minutes).
11. Place on a wire rack to cool completely.
12. Meanwhile, prepare the cream cheese frosting. Cream the cheese using a mixer until fluffy. Mix in powdered sugar to incorporate. Add lemon juice and mix at low speed until smooth.
13. Frost cooled loaf and serve.

Calories 420,
Total Fat 17 gr.
Carbs 61 gr
Protein 6 gr

Classic Cheesecake
from the Cheesecake Factory

Difficulty ● ○ ○

Cost $ $ $

Servings 12

Preparation Time............ 4 h 15 m

Cooking Time................... 1 h 5 m

Crust:
- 1 1/2 cups graham cracker crumbs
- 1/4 teaspoon cinnamon, ground
- 1/3 cup margarine, melted

Filling:
- 4 8-ounce packages cream cheese, softened
- 1 1/4 cups white sugar
- 1/2 cup sour cream
- 2 teaspoons vanilla extract
- 5 large eggs

Topping:
- 1/2 cup sour cream
- 2 teaspoons sugar

No matter how many versions of cheesecakes the famous restaurant invents, the original cheesecake will always have a special place in our hearts—and now in our recipe lists.

1. Preheat oven to 475°F and heat a large skillet with 1/2 inch water inside.
2. Combine ingredients for the crust in a bowl. In a large pie pan lined with parchment paper, spread crust onto pan and press firmly. Cover with foil and keep in freezer until ready to use.
3. Combine ingredients for the filling, except for eggs, in a bowl. Scrape bowl while beating, until mixture is smooth. Mix in eggs and beat until fully blended.
4. Take out crust from freezer and add filling onto crust, spreading evenly. Place pie pan into heated water bath (skillet in oven) and bake for about 12 minutes. Reduce heat to 350 °F. Continue to bake for about 50 minutes or until cake top is golden. Remove from oven and transfer skillet onto a wire rack to cool.
5. Prepare the topping by mixing all ingredients in a bowl. Coat cake with topping, then cover. Keep inside refrigerator for at least 4 hours.
6. Serve cold.

Calories 519,
Total Fat 39 gr.
Carbs 34 gr.
Protein 10 gr.

Cracker Barrel's Double Fudge Coca Cola Chocolate Cake

Difficulty ●●○

Cost $ $ $

Servings 12

Preparation Time............ 20 min

Cooking Time.................. 40 min

Cake:
- Non-stick cooking spray
- 1/2 cup unsalted butter
- 1/2 cup vegetable oil
- 3 tablespoons unsweetened cocoa powder
- 1 cup Coca Cola™
- 2 cups all-purpose flour
- 2 cups granulated sugar
- 1/2 teaspoon salt
- 1 teaspoon baking soda

- 1/2 cup buttermilk
- 1 teaspoon pure vanilla extract
- 2 eggs

Frosting:
- 1/2 cup unsalted butter (1 stick), softened
- 1 teaspoon pure vanilla extract
- 3 tablespoons unsweetened cocoa powder
- 6 tablespoons Coca Cola™
- 4 cups powdered sugar

1. Preheat oven to 350°F. Coat a large rectangular 9x13-inch baking pan with non-stick cooking spray.
2. Add the butter, oil, cocoa powder, and Coca Cola™ to a saucepan. Bring to a boil. Add mixture to the electric beater bowl. Add the sugar, flour, salt, and baking powder. Beat on medium speed until well combined.
3. Add one egg at a time. Add buttermilk and vanilla. Beat until well combined and cake batter is smooth.
4. Transfer prepared batter into pan, spreading evenly. Place in oven and bake for 40 minutes.
5. While the cake is in the oven, prepare the frosting. Using an electric beater, beat the butter into cream. Add 6 tablespoons of Coca Cola™, cocoa powder and vanilla. Beat until well combined.
6. Add the powdered sugar by increment of 1 cup at a time. Beat until frosting is smooth and fluffy.
7. Bring cake out of oven. While cake is still hot, spread the chocolate frosting evenly over the cake. Let cool down before covering with a plastic paper and place in the refrigerator until ready to serve. Serve with a scoop of vanilla ice cream, if desired.

Calories 755,
Total Fat 25 gr.
Carbs 108 gr.
Protein 5 gr.

Chili's Molten Lava Cake

Difficulty ● ● ○

Cost $ $ $

Servings 16

Preparation Time............ 75 min

Cooking Time.................. 30 min

- 1 14-ounce can sweetened condensed milk
- 12-ounce bag plus 1 cup semi-sweet chocolate chips, divided
- 4 tablespoons unsalted butter
- 1 teaspoon pure vanilla extract
- 1 pinch salt
- 1 package fudge cake mix
- 3 large eggs
- 1/2 cup sour cream
- 1 cup milk
- 1/2 cup canola oil
- Non-stick cooking spray
- 1 cup milk chocolate chips
- 1/4 cup coconut oil
- Vanilla ice cream
- Caramel syrup

1. Make hot fudge by adding condensed milk, 1 bag chocolate chips, butter, vanilla extract, and salt to a saucepan over medium heat, stirring frequently. Once boiling, continue for about 2 minutes. Turn off heat but keep stirring mixture for 1 minute more. Set aside to cool.
2. Combine cake mix, eggs, sour cream, milk, and oil in a bowl. Set aside.
3. Coat a molten cake pan or a cupcake pan with non-stick cooking spray, then pour batter into each mold. Leave about 1/4 mold without batter. Bake based on package instructions. Then, invert cakes to form volcano shape then let cool.
4. Carefully cut some cake out off center of each, in a cone shape, but not all the way through. Pour cooled hot fudge into hole. Taking the cut off cake layer, cut a thin slice on largest part then position above hot fudge like a cap.
5. As cake cools, prepare magic shells by microwaving a bowl of coconut oil and remaining chocolate chips in 30-second intervals, stirring after every interval, until melted. Wait to cool.
6. Serve cakes on a plate and top with ice cream followed by caramel, then magic shell.

Carraba's Dessert Rosa

Difficulty ● ● ●

Cost $ $ $

Servings 12

Preparation Time............ 20 min

Cooking Time.................. 40 min

- 1 box white cake mix
- 1 stick butter
- 6 egg yolks
- 1/2 cup sugar, divided
- 4 tablespoons all-purpose flour
- 1 pinch salt
- 2 cups milk
- 3 teaspoons vanilla extract, divided
- 8 strawberries, sliced

- 2 bananas, sliced
- 1 can crushed pineapple
- 1 cup heavy cream
- 1/4 cup sugar
- 1 teaspoon vanilla extract
- Chocolate syrup

1. Make cake according to package instructions but replace oil with butter. Then, set aside to cool.
2. Start making pastry cream by adding egg yolks and 1/4 cup sugar to a bowl. Mix until smooth and liquid becomes lighter in color. Stir in flour and salt until combined. Set aside.
3. Heat milk, remaining sugar, and 2 teaspoons vanilla extract in a saucepan over medium heat. Bring to a boil. Then, while stirring, gradually pour about half of scalding milk mixture into egg yolk/sugar mixture. Return saucepan to heat and pour in egg yolk/sugar mixture. Continue to stir until sauce comes to a boil Continue boiling for about 1 minute or until cream thickens, stirring continuously. Turn off heat, then pour into a bowl. Mix in butter until melted. Cover with bowl with plastic wrap and refrigerate for 1 hour.
4. For the fruit topping, add strawberries and bananas into individual bowls, unmixed, and pour in juice of canned pineapples. Add pineapples to a separate bowl. For whipped cream, whisk heavy cream in a bowl until a bit firm. Whisk in sugar and remaining vanilla extract until you can form a firm peak.
5. Assemble cake by slicing it into two layers. Return 1st layer onto pan, then layer with pineapple and pastry cream. Top with 2nd cake layer, then top with strawberries, followed by bananas. Drizzle chocolate syrup on top.
6. Right before serving, spread whipped cream onto individual cake slices.

The Cheesecake Factory's Copycat Ultimate Red Velvet Cheesecake

Difficulty ●○○

Cost $ $ $

Servings 16

Preparation Time............ 3 h 30 min

Cooking Time.................... 1 h 15 min

Cheesecake:
- 8-ounce packages cream cheese, softened
- 2/3 cup granulated white sugar
- 1 pinch salt
- 2 large eggs
- 1/3 cup sour cream
- 1/3 cup heavy whipping cream
- 1 teaspoon vanilla extract
- Non-stick cooking spray
- Hot water, for water bath

Red velvet cake:
- 2 1/2 cups all-purpose flour

1 1/2 cups granulated white sugar

- 3 tablespoons unsweetened cocoa powder
- 1 1/2 teaspoons baking soda
- 1 teaspoon salt
- 2 large eggs
- 1 1/2 cups vegetable oil
- 1 cup buttermilk
- 1/4 cup red food coloring
- 2 teaspoons vanilla extract
- 2 teaspoons white vinegar

Frosting:
- 2 1/2 cups powdered sugar, sifted
- 2 8-ounce packages cream cheese, softened
- 1/2 cup unsalted butter, softened
- 1 tablespoon vanilla extract

1. For the cheesecake, preheat oven to 325°F.
2. Mix cream cheese, sugar, and salt using a mixer for about 2 minutes until creamy and smooth. Add eggs, mixing again after adding each one. Add sour cream, heavy cream, and vanilla extract until smooth and well blended.
3. Coat spring form pan with non-stick cooking spray, then place parchment paper on top. Wrap outsides of Spring Form pan entirely with two layers of aluminum foil. This is prevent water bath from entering the pan.
4. Pour cream cheese batter into Spring Form pan, then place into a roasting pan. Add boiling water to roasting pan to surround Spring Form pan. Place in oven and bake for 45 minutes until set.
5. Transfer Spring Form pan with cheesecake onto a rack to cool for about 1 hour. Freeze overnight.
6. For the red velvet cake, preheat oven to 350°F.
7. Combine flour, sugar, cocoa powder, baking soda, and salt in a large bowl. In a separate bowl, mix eggs, oil, buttermilk, food coloring, vanilla and vinegar. Add wet ingredients to dry ingredients. Blend for 1 minute with a mixer on medium-low speed, then on high speed for 2 minutes.
8. Spray non-stick cooking spray to 2 metal baking pans that are the same size as the Spring Form pan earlier. Coat bottoms thinly with flour. Then, pour equal amounts cake batter onto bottom of pans.
9. Place in oven and bake for about 30 to 35 minutes. Cake is done once only a few crumbs attach to a toothpick when inserted. Transfer to a rack and let cool for 10 minutes. Separate cake from pan using a knife on the edges, then invert onto rack. Let cool.
10. To prepare frosting, mix powdered sugar, cream cheese, butter, and vanilla using a mixer on medium-high speed just enough until smooth.
11. Assemble cake by positioning 1st red velvet cake layer onto a cake plate. Remove cheesecake from pan, remove parchment paper, and layer on top of red velvet cake layer. Then, top with 2nd red velvet cake layer.
12. Coat a thin layer of prepared frosting onto entire outside of cake. Clean spatula every time you scoop out from bowl of frosting so as to not mix crumbs into it. Refrigerate for 30 minutes to set. Then, coat cake with 2nd layer by adding a large scoop on top then spreading it to the top side of the cake then around it.
13. Cut into slices. Serve.

Dinner

Chipotle Chicken

Difficulty ● ● ○

Cost $ $ $

Servings 8

Preparation Time............ 10 min

Cooking Time.................. 20 min

- 1/2 pound organic boneless and skinless chicken breasts or thighs
- Olive oil or cooking spray

Marinade
- 7 oz. chipotle peppers in adobo sauce
- 2 tablespoons olive oil

- 6 garlic cloves, peeled
- 1 teaspoon black pepper
- 2 teaspoons salt
- 1/2 teaspoon cumin
- 1/2 teaspoon dry oregano

1. Pour all the marinade ingredients in a food processor or blender and blend until you get a smooth paste.
2. Pound the chicken until it has a thickness between 1/2 to ¾ inch. Place chicken into an airtight container or re-sealable plastic bag such as a Ziploc. Pour the marinade over the chicken and stir until well coated. Place the chicken in the refrigerator and let marinate overnight or up to 24 hours.
3. Pour the blended mixture into the container and marinate the chicken for at least 8 hours.
4. Cook the chicken over medium to high heat on an oiled and preheated grill for 3 to 5 minutes per side. The internal temperature of the chicken should be 165 Fahrenheit before you remove it from the heat. You can also cook it in a heavy-bottomed skillet over medium heat with a little olive oil.
5. Let rest before serving. If desired, cut into cubes to add to salads, tacos, or quesadillas or serve as is.

Calories 293,
Fat 18.7 gr.
Carbs 5.8 gr.
Protein 24.9 gr.

Longhorns Parmesan Crusted Chicken

Difficulty ●●○

Cost $ $ $

Servings 4

Preparation Time........... 10 min

Cooking Time.................. 30 min

- 4 chicken breasts, skinless
- 2 teaspoons salt
- 2 teaspoons ground black pepper
- 2 tablespoons avocado oil

For the Marinade:
- 1 tablespoon minced garlic
- 1/2 teaspoon ground black pepper
- 1 teaspoon juice
- 3 tablespoon Worcester sauce

- 1 teaspoon white vinegar
- 1/2 cup avocado oil
- 1/2 cup ranch dressing

For the Parmesan Crust:
- 1 cup panko breadcrumbs 6 ounces parmesan chees chopped
- 5 tablespoons melted butter, unsalted
- 6 ounces provolone cheese, chopped
- 2 teaspoons garlic powder
- 6 tablespoons ranch dressing, low-carb

1. Prepare the marinade and for this, take a little bowl, place all of its ingredients in it then whisk until well combined. Pound each chicken until ¾-inch thick, then season with salt and black pepper and transfer chicken pieces to an outsized bag.
2. Pour within the prepared marinade, seal the bag, turn it upside to coat chicken with it and let it rest for a minimum of half-hour within the refrigerator.
3. Then take an outsized skillet pan, place it over medium-high heat, add oil and when hot, place marinated pigeon breast in it then cook for five minutes per side until chicken is not any longer pink and nicely seared on all sides.
4. Transfer chicken to a plate and repeat it with the remaining chicken pieces. Meanwhile, turn on the oven, set it to 450 degrees F, and let it preheat.
5. When the chicken has cooked, prepare the parmesan crust and for this, take a little heatproof bowl, place both cheeses in it, pour in ranch dressing and milk, stir until mixed, then microwave for 30 seconds. Then stir the cheese mixture again until smooth and continue microwaving for an additional 15 seconds.
6. Stir the cheese mixture again, spread evenly on top of every pigeon breast, arrange them during a baking sheet then bake for five minutes until cheese has melted.
7. Meanwhile, take a little bowl, place breadcrumbs in it, stir in garlic powder and butter in it. After 5 minutes of baking, spread the breadcrumbs mixture on top of the chicken then continue baking for two minutes until the panko mixture turns brown. Serve chicken immediately with cauliflower mashed potatoes.

Carrabba Pollo Rosa Maria

Difficulty ● ● ○

Cost $ $ $

Servings 8

Preparation Time........... 10 min

Cooking Time.................. 50 min

- 4 butterflied chicken breasts
- 4 slices prosciutto
- 4 slices Fontina cheese
- 1/2 cup clarified butter
- 3 garlic cloves
- 1/2 sweet onion, diced
- 1/4 cup dry white wine

- 4 tablespoons unsalted butter
- 1/2 white pepper
- 1 dash salt
- 8 ounces cremini mushrooms, sliced
- 1/2 cup fresh basil, chopped
- 1 lemon, juiced
- Shredded Parmesan for garnish

1. Grill the chicken breasts on each side for 3 to 5 minutes.
2. Remove the chicken from heat and then stuff with the prosciutto and cheese. Place the ham and cheese on one side of the chicken and fold it over. Secure the filling with a toothpick.
3. Wrap the chicken in foil to keep it warm.
4. Sauté the onions and garlic in butter until they become tender. Add the white wine to deglaze the pan.
5. In the same pan, sauté the mushrooms in the salt, pepper, and butter until tender, then add the remaining ingredients and cook until completely blended.
6. Transfer the chicken to a plate and pour the mushroom sauce over it. Remove the toothpick and serve. Garnish with Parmesan cheese, if desired

Calories 644,
Fat 52.3 gr.
Carbs 6 gr.
Protein 36 gr.

Panda Express Kung Pao Chicken

Difficulty ● ● ○

Cost $ $ $

Servings 10

Preparation Time............ 10 min

Cooking Time................... 30 min

- 35 ounces chicken thighs, skinless
- 1/2-inch cubed 14 ounces zucchini, destemmed
- 1/2-inch diced 14 ounces red bell pepper, cored
- 1-inch cubed 1 scallion, sliced
- 15 pieces of dried Chinese red peppers
- 1 1/2 teaspoons minced garlic
- 1 teaspoon minced ginger
- 3 ounces roasted peanuts
- 1/4 teaspoon ground black pepper

- 1/4 teaspoon xanthan gum
- 3 tablespoons copra oil
- 1 tablespoon balsamic vinegar
- 1 tablespoon chili aioli
- ¾ tablespoon vegetable oil

For the Marinade:
- 3 tablespoons coconut aminos
- 1 tablespoon copra oil
- For the Sauce:
- 3 tablespoons monk fruit sweetener
- 3 tablespoons coconut aminos

1. Marinade the chicken and for this, take an outsized bowl, place the chicken pieces in it, then add all the ingredients for the marinade in it. Stir until chicken is well coated then marinate for a minimum of half-hour within the refrigerator.

2. Then take an outsized skillet pan, add 1 tablespoon of copra oil in it and when it melted, add marinated chicken and cook for 10 minutes or more until it starts to release its water.

3. After 10 minutes, push the chicken to the edges of the pan to make a well in its middle, slowly stir in xanthan gum into the water released by chicken and cook for two to 4 minutes until it starts to thicken.

4. Then stir chicken into the thicken liquid and continue cooking for 10 minutes or more until chicken has thoroughly cooked, put aside until required. Return pan over medium-high heat, add 1 tablespoon oil, and when it melts, add bell pepper and zucchini cubes then cook for five to eight minutes until lightly browned.

5. Transfer vegetables to a separate plate, then add remaining copra oil into the pan, add Chinese red peppers, ginger, garlic, vinegar, and chili aioli. Stir until mixed, cook for 3 minutes, add ingredients for the sauce alongside peanuts, scallion, black pepper, and vegetable oil and continue cooking for 3 minutes, stirring frequently. Return chicken and vegetables into the pan, toss until well mixed then continue cooking for 3 to five minutes until hot. Serve immediately.

Olive Garden Parmesan Crusted Chicken

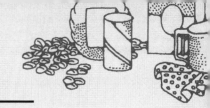

Difficulty ●●○

Cost $ $ $

Servings 4

Preparation Time............ 15 min

Cooking Time.................... 40 min

Breading
- 1 cup plain breadcrumbs
- 2 tablespoons flour
- 1/4 cup grated parmesan cheese

For dipping
- 1 cup milk
- Chicken
- 2 chicken breasts
- Vegetable oil for frying
- 2 cups cooked linguini pasta
- 2 tablespoons butter
- 3 tablespoons olive oil

- 2 teaspoons crushed garlic
- 1/2 cup white wine
- 1/4 cup water
- 2 tablespoons flour
- ¾ cup half-and-half
- 1/4 cup sour cream
- 1/2 teaspoon salt
- 1 teaspoon fresh flat leave parsley, finely diced ¾ cup mild Asiago cheese, finely grated
- Garnish
- 1 Roma tomato, diced
- Grated parmesan cheese
- Fresh flat-leaf parsley, finely chopped

1. Pound the chicken until it flattens to 1/2 inch thick.
2. Mix the breading ingredients in one shallow bowl and place the milk in another.
3. Heat some oil over medium to medium-to-low heat.
4. Dip the chicken in the breading, then the milk, then the breading again. Immediately place into the heated oil.
5. Cook the chicken in the oil until golden brown, about 3-4 minutes per side. Remove the chicken and set aside on a plate lined with paper towels.
6. Create a roux by adding flour to heated olive oil and butter over medium heat.
7. When the roux is done, add the garlic, water, and salt to the pan and stir.
8. Add the wine and continue stirring and cooking.
9. Add the half-and-half and sour cream and stir some more.
10. Add the cheese and let it melt.
11. Finally, add in the parsley and remove from heat. Add pasta and stir to coat.
12. Divide the hot pasta between serving plates.
13. Top each dish with the chicken, diced tomatoes, and parmesan cheese before serving.

Olive Garden Chicken Marsala

Difficulty ● ○ ○

Cost $ $ $

Servings 4-6

Preparation Time............ 10 min

Cooking Time.................... 40 min

- 2 tablespoons olive oil
- 2 tablespoons butter
- 4 boneless skinless chicken breasts
- 1 1/2 cups sliced mushrooms
- 1 small clove garlic, thinly sliced
- Flour for dredging

- Sea salt and freshly ground black pepper
- 1 1/2 cups chicken stock
- 1 1/2 cups Marsala wine
- 1 tablespoon lemon juice
- 1 teaspoon Dijon mustard

1. Chicken scaloppini:
2. Pound out the chicken with a mallet or rolling pin to about 1/2 inch thick
3. In a large skillet, heat the olive oil and 1 tablespoon of the butter over medium-high heat. When the oil is hot, dredge the chicken in flour. Season with salt and pepper on both sides. Dredge only as many as will fit in the skillet. Don't overcrowd the pan.
4. Cook chicken in batches, about 1 to 2 minutes on each side or until cooked through. Remove from skillet, and place on an oven-proof platter. Keep warm, in the oven, while the rest of the chicken is cooking.
5. Marsala sauce:
6. In the same skillet, add 1 tablespoon of olive oil. On medium-high heat, sauté mushrooms and garlic until softened. Remove the mushrooms from the pan and set aside.
7. Add the chicken stock and loosen any remaining bits in the pan. On high heat, let reduce by half, about 6-8 minutes. Add Marsala wine and lemon juice and in the same manner reduce by half, about 6-8 minutes. Add the mushroom back in the saucepan, and stir in the Dijon mustard. Warm for 1 minute on medium-low heat. Remove from heat, stir in the remaining butter to make the sauce silkier. To serve, pour the sauce over chicken, and serve immediately.

Calories 970,
Fat 43g,
Carbs 71g,
Protein 66 g

KFC Fried Chicken

Difficulty ●○○

Cost $ $ $

Servings 6

Preparation Time............ 15 min

Cooking Time................... 18 min

For the Seasoning:
- 1 teaspoon flavorer
- 1 teaspoon of sea salt
- 1 teaspoon ginger powder
- 1 tablespoon ground white pepper
- 2 teaspoons flavorer
- 1 teaspoon ground black pepper
- 4 teaspoons paprika
- 1/4 teaspoon dried oregano
- 1/2 teaspoon dried thyme

- 1 teaspoon mustard powder

For the Marinade:
- 1/2 of the seasoning
- 4 tablespoons white vinegar
- 3 tablespoons cream 2 cups almond milk, unsweetened
- 2 eggs

For the Chicken:
- 8 1/2 cups avocado oil
- 2 pounds of chicken drumsticks
- 2 1/2 cups whey protein powder

1. Prepare the seasoning and for this, take a little bowl, place all of its ingredients in it then stir until mixed, put aside until required. Prepare the marinade and for this, take an outsized bowl, pour in milk, add vinegar and cream, whisk until blended then let it sit for 10 minutes.
2. Then whisk in eggs until combined, and whisk in 1/2 of seasoning until smooth. Place chicken pieces into an outsized bag, pour within the marinade, seal the bag, turn it the wrong way up to coat chicken then let it marinate within the refrigerator for a minimum of 4 hours.
3. Cook the chicken, and for this, take an outsized pan, place it over medium heat, pour within the oil, and warmth it for 12 minutes or more until the temperature reaches 325 degrees F. Spread remaining seasoning mixture on a plate, take a chicken piece, coat it with the seasoning mix then add into the pan.
4. Add more seasoned chicken pieces into the pan until filled and cook for 16 to 18 minutes until the interior temperature of chicken reaches 165 degrees F and turns nicely browned, turning chicken frequently. When done, transfer fried chicken to a plate lined with paper towels, then repeat with the remaining chicken pieces. Serve immediately.

Calories 590.2;
Fats 39.6g;
Protein 57.6 g;
Carb 1.1g

Addy's Bar and GrillBuffalo wings

Difficulty ●○○

Cost $ $ $

Servings 3

Preparation Time............ 45 min

Cooking Time................... 10 min

- 12 chicken wings, frozen
- 1/2 teaspoon salt
- 1/4 teaspoon ground black pepper
- 1/2 cup avocado oil

- For the Sauce:
- 1/2 tablespoon minced garlic
- 1/4 teaspoon paprika
- 1/4 teaspoon cayenne pepper
- 4 tablespoons butter, salted
- 1/4 cup sauce, low-carb

1. Switch on the oven, then set it to 400 degrees F and let it preheat. Meanwhile, take an outsized baking dish, spread chicken wings thereon, rub them with oil, and then sprinkle with salt and black pepper.
2. Bake the chicken wings for 45 minutes until crisp, turning halfway through. Meanwhile, prepare the sauce and for this, take a little saucepan, place it over medium-low heat, add butter and garlic and cook for 3 to five minutes until butter melts.
3. Add remaining ingredients for the sauce, whisk until combined, cook for two minutes until hot, and then remove pan from heat. Add baked chicken wings into the sauce then toss until well coated. Serve immediately.

Calories 391;
Fats 32g;
Protein 31g;
Carb 1g

Tso Chicken

Difficulty ●●○

Cost $ $ $

Servings 4

Preparation Time........... 10 min

Cooking Time.................. 20 min

- **For the Chicken:**
- **1 1/2 pounds chicken thighs, boneless**
- **1 scallion, chopped**
- **1/2 cup almond flour**
- **1/4 teaspoon salt**
- **1/4 teaspoon ground black pepper**
- **1/2 teaspoon xanthan gum**
- **2 egg whites**
- **2 tablespoons copra oil**
- **1/2 cup chicken stock**
- **1 teaspoon sesame seeds For the Sauce:**
- **1 1/2 tablespoon minced garlic**
- **1/2 teaspoon grated ginger**
- **1 teaspoon Swerve sweetener**
- **1 teaspoon red chili paste**
- **5 tablespoons soy**
- **2 tablespoons ketchup, sugar-free**
- **1 teaspoon vegetable oil**

1. **Prepare the sauce and for this, take a medium bowl, place all of its ingredients in it then whisk until combined, put aside until required. Prepare the chicken and for this, cut it into bite-size pieces then season it with salt and black pepper.**
2. **Take a shallow dish, crack the egg in it and whisk until frothy. Take a separate shallow dish then spread flour in it. Working on one chicken piece at a time, first dip it into the egg, dredge it into the flour until coated, and repeat with the remaining pieces.**
3. **Plug-in the moment pot, press the 'sauté' button, add oil and when hot, add chicken pieces during a single layer then cook them for 3 to 4 minutes per side until golden brown.**
4. **Transfer the chicken pieces to a plate and repeat with the remaining chicken pieces. When done, stir broth into the inner pot to get rid of browned bits from rock bottom of the pot, return chicken pieces into the pot and pour the prepared sauce over them.**
5. **Shut the moment pot with its lid within the sealed position, press the manual button, and let the chicken cook for 4 minutes. When the moment pot, do a fast pressure release, then open the moment pot and stir xanthan gum into the chicken until sauce thickens. Top chicken with sesame seeds and green onions and serve with cauliflower rice.**

Calories 427;
Fats 30g;
Protein 35g;
Carb 1g

Applebee Fiesta Lime Chicken

Difficulty ●○○

Cost $ $ $

Servings 4

Preparation Time............ 10 min

Cooking Time.................. 13 min

- 1 pound pigeon breast
- 1 cup shredded Colby-Monterey jack cheese

For the Marinade:
- 1 1/2 teaspoon minced garlic
- 1/4 teaspoon ginger powder
- 1/2 teaspoon salt
- 1 teaspoon liquid smoke
- 1/2 of lime, juiced
- 1/3 cup teriyaki sauce
- 1 teaspoon tequila
- 1 cup of water

For the Dressing:
- 1 teaspoon Cajun spice mix
- 1/4 teaspoon dried parsley
- 1/8 teaspoon cumin
- 1/8 teaspoon dried dill
- 1/4 teaspoon sauce
- 2 tablespoons spicy salsa, low-carb
- 1 tablespoon coconut milk, unsweetened
- 1/4 cup soured cream
- 1/4 cup mayonnaise

1. Prepare the marinade and for this, take an outsized bowl, place all of its ingredients in it then whisk until combined. Add chicken, toss until well coated then let the chicken marinate within the refrigerator for a minimum of two hours.
2. Meanwhile, prepare the dressing and for this, take an outsized bowl, place all of its ingredients in it, whisk until combined, and let it rest within the refrigerator until chilled.
3. When the chicken has marinated, found out the grill and let it preheat at a high heat setting for five minutes.
4. Place chicken on the cooking grate then cook it for five minutes per side until thoroughly cooked.
5. When done, brush the chicken generously with prepared dressing, arrange chicken during a baking sheet, and sprinkle cheese on top, then broil for 3 minutes until cheese has melted.
6. Serve chicken immediately.

Nutrition:
Calories 294;
Fat 14.5g;
Protein 33.2g;
Carb 6.1g

Garcia Pollo Fundido

Difficulty ●○○

Cost $ $ $

Servings 4

Preparation Time............ 10 min

Cooking Time................... 45 min

- 2 pounds of chicken breasts
- 4 ounces diced green chilies
- 1/2 teaspoon garlic powder
- 1/4 teaspoon of sea salt
- 1/4 teaspoon ground black pepper
- 1/4 teaspoon cumin
- 8 ounces cheese, softened
- 1 cup Monterrey jack cheese

1. Switch on the oven, then set it to 375 degrees F and let it preheat. Meanwhile, take an outsized bowl, place cheese in it, add all the seasoning and spices, stir well until well combined, and then fold within the green chilies until incorporated.
2. Take an outsized baking dish, place chicken breasts in it with some space between them, and spread cheese mixture on the highest evenly. Sprinkle cheese on the highest then bake for 45 minutes until the chicken has thoroughly cooked. When done, let the chicken cool for five minutes then serve.

Calories 520;
Fats 25g;
Protein 62g;
Carb 5g

Popeye Chicken Strips

Difficulty ● ○ ○

Cost $ $ $

Servings 6

Preparation Time............ 10 min

Cooking Time................... 20 min

- **2 pounds of chicken breasts**
- **2/3 cup almond flour**
- **2 teaspoons salt**
- **1 teaspoon chipotle flavorer**
- **2 teaspoons smoked paprika**
- **1/3 cup Louisiana style sauce , low-carb 3 eggs**
- **1/2 cup almond milk, unsweetened**
- **Avocado oil as required for frying**

1. Take a little bowl, pour within the milk, and then whisk in sauce. Cut each pigeon breast into four strips, place them into an outsized bowl, pour in half the milk mixture, and then marinate for a minimum of 1 hour.
2. Then take a shallow dish, place flour in it, and stir in salt, paprika, and chipotle until mixed. Crack the eggs into the remaining milk mixture then whisk until frothy.
3. When the chicken has marinated, drain it well, dredge each chicken strip into the flour mixture, read the egg mixture and dredge again in flour mixture. When able to cook, take an outsized skillet pan, fill it 2 1/2-inches of oil, place the pan over medium-high heat and convey the oil to 360 degrees F.
4. Then lower the chicken pieces into the oil, don't overcrowd it, and then cook for five to 7 minutes per side until cooked and golden brown. Transfer chicken pieces to a plate lined with paper towels then repeat with the remaining chicken pieces. Serve immediately.

Calories 385;
Fats 25g,
Protein 35g;
Carb 4g

Olive Garden Chicken Piccata

Difficulty ● ○ ○

Cost $ $ $

Servings 5

Preparation Time............ 10 min

Cooking Time.................. 15 min

- 2 pounds chicken breasts, thinly sliced
- 2 tablespoons chopped parsley
- 1/4 cup drained capers, rinsed
- 1/2 teaspoon salt
- 1/2 teaspoon ground black pepper
- 1/3 cup juice
- 2 tablespoons avocado oil
- 4 tablespoons butter, unsalted, divided
- 1/2 cup chicken stock

1. Prepare the chicken and for this, pound the chicken with a meat mallet then season with salt and black pepper.
2. Take an outsized skillet pan, place it over medium-high heat, add oil and a couple of tablespoons of butter and when hot, add chicken until the pan is filled then cook for two minutes per side until nicely golden brown.
3. When done, transfer chicken to a plate then repeat with the remaining chicken.
4. When done, stir juice and broth into the pan to get rid of browned bits from the pan, add capers then bring the mixture to a boil.
5. Return chicken into the pan, simmer for two minutes, and then transfer chicken pieces to a plate.
6. Add remaining butter into the pan, whisk it until combined, then drizzle the sauce over chicken. Garnish the chicken with parsley then serve.

Calories 385;
Fats 25g;
Protein 35g;
Carb 4g

Cheesecake Factory Tuna Tataki Salad

Difficulty ●○○

Cost $ $ $

Servings 4

Preparation Time............ 10 min

Cooking Time................... 5 min

- 1 pound tuna, sashimi grade
- 4 tablespoons avocado oil

For the Salad:
- 4 radishes, peeled, sliced thinly
- 8 cups salad greens
- 4 green onion, sliced
- 4 avocados, peeled, pitted, sliced
- 2 teaspoons black sesame seeds

For the Salad Dressing:
- 2 1-inch pieces of ginger, grated
- 2 tablespoons liquid stevia
- 4 tablespoons ponzu sauce, low-carb
- 2 tablespoons sake
- 2 tablespoons soy sauce
- 2 tablespoons toasted sesame oil

1. Prepare the salad dressing and for this, take a mason jar, place all of its ingredients in it, shut with the lid, and then shake well until well blended, set aside until required.

2. Take a large salad bowl, place avocado slices, radish, and salad greens in it, and then toss until mixed. Prepare the tuna and for this, take a large skillet pan, place it over medium heat, add oil and when hot, add tuna and then cook for 1 minute per side until seared.

3. Transfer tuna to a plate, repeat with the remaining tuna, let cool for 15 minutes and then cut tuna into thin slices. Distribute salad evenly among four plates, add seared tuna to the side and then drizzle with prepared salad dressing. Sprinkle sesame seeds and green onion over tuna and then serve.

Calories 594;
Fat 42.2g;
Protein 37.1g;
Carb 4.4g

Outback Steakhouse Coconut Shrimp

Difficulty ● ○ ○

Cost $ $ $

Servings 4

Preparation Time........... 14 min

Cooking Time.................. 10 min

- 1 pound medium shrimp, tail removed, peeled, deveined, cooked
- 1/2 cup pork rind
- 1 teaspoon salt
- 1/2 cup shredded coconut, unsweetened
- 1/2 teaspoon ground black pepper
- 1/4 cup coconut milk, unsweetened

1. Take a shallow pan, place it over low heat and when hot, add coconut and cook for 3 to 4 minutes until golden brown. Take a shallow dish, and then pour in the milk. Take a separate shallow dish, place coconut and pork rind in it, and then stir until mixed. Pat dry the shrimp with paper towels then dip each shrimp into milk and dredge in the pork-coconut mixture until evenly coated. Plugin the air fryer, insert a greased fryer basket, set it 400 degrees F, and let it preheat for 400 degrees F.

2. Then add shrimps in a single layer into the fryer basket and then fry for 7 minutes, shaking halfway. When done, transfer fried shrimps to a plate and repeat with the remaining shrimps. Season the shrimps with salt and black pepper and then serve.

Calories 335;
Fat15.6g;
Protein 46.1g;
Carb 0.9g

Cheesecake Factory Bang Bang Shrimp

Difficulty	●○○	
Cost	$ $ $	
Servings	4	

Preparation Time............ 14 min

Cooking Time................... 12 min

For the Shrimp:
- 1 pound shrimp, tail removed, peeled, deveined
- 1/2 cup coconut flour
- Avocado oil as needed for frying

1 scallion, sliced

For the Sauce:
- 1/3 cup mayonnaise
- 1 ¾ tablespoon garlic chili sauce
- 1 1/2 tablespoon rice vinegar
- 2 1/2 tablespoons monk fruit Sweetener
- 1/8 teaspoon salt

1. Prepare the shrimps and for this, dredge each shrimp in coconut flour and then arrange on a baking sheet. Then take a large skillet pan, place it over medium-high heat, fill it 2-inch with oil and when hot, add shrimps in it and then cook for 4 minutes or more until pink.
2. When done, transfer shrimps to a plate lined with paper towels and repeat with the remaining shrimps. Prepare the sauce and for this, plug in a food processor, add all the ingredients in it, cover with the lid and then pulse for 30 seconds until smooth.
3. Tip the sauce into a large bowl, add shrimps and then toss until coated. Garnish shrimps with scallion and then serve.

Calories 204;
Fat 16g;
Protein 20g;
Carb 3g

ockside Grill Restaurant Fish Cakes

Difficulty ●○○

Cost $ $ $

Servings 2

Preparation Time............ 14 min

Cooking Time.................. 15 min

For the Fish Cake:
- 1 pound white fish, boneless
- 1/4 cup cilantro leaves
- 1/4 teaspoon salt
- 1/4 teaspoon red chili flakes
- 1 tablespoon minced garlic
- 2 tablespoons avocado oil

For the Dip:
- 1 lemon, juiced
- 2 avocados, peeled, pitted
- 1/4 teaspoon salt
- 2 tablespoons water

1. Prepare the fish cakes and for this, place all of its ingredients in a food processor except for oil and then pulse for 3 minutes until well combined.
2. Tip the mixture in a large bowl and then shape it into six patties.
3. Take a frying pan, place it over medium-high heat, add oil and when hot, add fish patties in it and then cook for 3 to 4 minutes per side until cooked and golden brown.
4. Meanwhile, prepare the dip and for this, place all of its ingredients in a food processor and then pulse for 2 minutes until smooth.
5. Serve fish cakes with prepared dip.

Calories 175;
Fats 9.7g;
Protein 9.1g;
Carb 13g

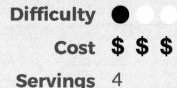

Whole Foods California Quinoa Salad

Difficulty ●○○

Cost $ $ $

Servings 4

Preparation Time............ 10 min

Cooking Time.................. 10 min

- 2 cups water
- 1 cup quinoa
- 1/4 cup balsamic vinegar
- 2 tablespoons lime zest
- 1 mango, peeled and finely chopped
- 1 red bell pepper, finely chopped

- 1/2 cup pre-cooked edamame, peeled
- 1/3 cup red onion, diced
- 1/4 cup unsweetened coconut flakes
- 1/4 cup almonds, chopped
- 1/4 cup raisins
- 2 tablespoons cilantro leaves, diced

1. In a skillet, cook quinoa with water according to package directions.
2. Meanwhile, combine balsamic vinegar and lime zest in a bowl.
3. In a separate bowl, mix cooked quinoa, mango, bell pepper, edamame, red onion, coconut flakes, almonds, raisins, and cilantro.
4. Add vinegar and lime zest sauce onto quinoa salad. Toss to coat salad. Serve.

Calories 351;
Fat 10 g;
Carbs 57g;
Protein 11g

Boston Market Squash Casserole

Difficulty ●○○

Cost $ $ $

Servings 8

Preparation Time............ 15 min

Cooking Time.................. 20 min

- 1/2-ounce box corn muffin mix
- Vegetable oil for coating
- 4 1/2 cup zucchini, finely chopped
- 4 1/2 cup summer squash, finely chopped
- 1/3 cup butter
- 1 1/2 cups yellow onion, minced
- 1 teaspoon salt
- 1/2 teaspoon black pepper, ground
- 1/2 teaspoon thyme
- 1 tablespoon fresh parsley, sliced
- 2 chicken bouillon cubes
- 1 teaspoon garlic, finely chopped
- 8 ounces cheddar cheese, chopped

1. Preheat oven to 350°F and lightly coat baking tray with vegetable oil.
2. Follow package directions to cook corn muffins. Set aside.
3. In a deep pan, add zucchini and summer squash. Pour water into pan, enough to cover vegetables. Simmer over medium-low heat or until vegetables are soft. Add cooked squash mixture into a container along with 1 cup of the cooking water. Reserve for later. Discard remaining liquids.
4. Return pan to heat. Melt butter, and then stir-fry onions until fragrant. Add salt, pepper, thyme, and parsley. Stir in chicken bouillon cubes, garlic, cooked squash and zucchini mixture, and cheese. Sprinkle with crumbled corn muffins. Stir everything together until well-blended, then pour onto baking tray and cover with tinfoil.
5. Cook in oven for about 40 minutes. Remove cover and bake for an additional 20 minutes.
6. Serve hot.

Calories 397;
Fat 30g;
Carbs 23g;
Protein 11g

Ruth's Chris Sweet Potato Casserole

Difficulty ●○○

Cost $ $ $

Servings 6

Preparation Time............ 15 min

Cooking Time................... 1 h 20 min

- 2 large sweet potatoes covered in aluminum foil
- 1/3 cup plus 3 tablespoons butter, divided
- 2 tablespoons half and half
- Salt, to taste
- 1/2 cup brown sugar
- 1/4 cup all-purpose flour

1. Preheat oven to 350°F. Place sweet potatoes onto a baking tray and bake for about 60 minutes. Remove from oven.

2. In a bowl, add baked sweet potatoes, 3 tablespoons butter, half and half, and salt. Mash until well blended. In a separate bowl, combine pecans, brown sugar, flour, and remaining butter. Transfer mashed sweet potatoes into a casserole dish, then top with pecan mixture. Place in oven and bake for about 20 minutes until edges bubble and pecan topping is slightly brown. Serve.

Calories 416;
Fat 31g;
Carbs 42g;
Fibers 3g;
Protein 3g

Olive Garden Salad and Creamy Dressing

Difficulty ●○○

Cost $ $ $

Servings 4

Preparation Time............ 15 min

Cooking Time.................... 1 h 20 min

Dressing:
- 1 cup mayonnaise
- 2/3 cup white vinegar
- 5 teaspoons granulated sugar
- 2 tablespoons lemon juice
- 1 tablespoon water
- 2/3 cup Parmesan-Romano cheese blend
- 2 teaspoons olive oil
- 1 teaspoon Italian seasoning
- 1 teaspoon parsley flakes
- 1/2 teaspoon garlic salt

Salad:
- 1 bag salad blend of choice
- Red onion, sliced
- 16-20 pitted black olives, sliced
- Pepperoncini
- Roma tomato, sliced
- Croutons
- Parmesan cheese, shredded

1. To make the dressing, add mayonnaise, white vinegar, sugar, lemon juice, water, cheese blend, olive oil, Italian seasoning, parsley, and garlic salt to a blender. Pulse until well combined. Store in refrigerator.
2. Ready to serve after at least 2 hours.
3. Assemble salad by layering salad blend, red onion, black olives, pepperoni, tomato, croutons, and Parmesan cheese in a bowl.
4. Serve.

Calories 127.8;
Fat 10.2g;
Carbs 8.9g;
Protein 1.1g

Chipotle Copycat Cilantro Lime Rice

Difficulty ● ○ ○

Cost $ $ $

Servings 5

Preparation Time............ 15 min

Cooking Time................... 15 min

- 8 cups water
- 2 cups basmati rice, rinsed
- 2 1/4 teaspoons salt, divided
- 1 bay leaf
- 1 teaspoon olive oil
- 2 tablespoons cilantro, minced
- 2 tablespoons fresh lime juice
- 1 tablespoon fresh lemon juice

Add water to a pot and bring to a boil. Stir in rice, 2 teaspoons salt, and bay leaf. Let boil for 12 minutes. Discard bay leaf. Transfer to a serving bowl. Mix in cilantro, lime juice, and lemon juice. Season with remaining salt. Serve warm.

Calories 133.;
Fat 0.7g;
Carbs 26.1g;
Protein 4.5g

Panera Jalapeño-Cilantro Hummus

Difficulty ●○○

Cost $ $ $

Servings 16

Preparation Time............ 5 min

Cooking Time...................../

- 15-ounce cans chickpeas, rinsed and drained
- 2/3Cup tahini
- 2 garlic cloves, chopped
- 1 tablespoon lemon juice
- 1 teaspoon kosher salt
- 1/2 cup cilantro, leaves and stems
- 1 large jalapeño pepper, chopped
- ⅓ Cup water
- Extra-virgin olive oil
- Crackers of your choice

Add chickpeas, tahini, garlic, lemon juice, salt, cilantro, and jalapeño pepper to a food processor. Pulse until mixture turns smooth and has thickened. While still running, gradually add water until mixture gets an even and smoother consistency. Drizzle olive oil on top and serve with crackers on the side

Calories 126;
Fat 6g;
Carbs 15g;
Protein 5g

Cici Spinach-Alfredo Pizza

Difficulty ●○○

Cost $ $ $

Servings 6

Preparation Time............ 10 min

Cooking Time.................. 20 min

- 2 tablespoons butter
- 1/2 teaspoon salt
- 1/4 teaspoon black pepper
- ¾ cup heavy cream
- 3 ounces Romano cheese, shredded
- 1 pizza crust
- 1/2 package frozen spinach, thawed and drained
- 8 ounces mozzarella cheese, grated

Preheat oven to 450°F. Prepare Alfredo sauce by adding butter to a deep pan over medium heat. Once melted, add salt, pepper, and heavy cream. Bring to boil while stirring frequently. Remove from heat. Once sauce has cooled a bit, stir in Romano cheese until melted. Place pizza crust onto a baking tray. Thinly coat Alfredo sauce on crust then spread spinach over sauce. Sprinkle mozzarella evenly on top. Bake in oven for about 12 to 15 minutes until mozzarella is bubbling and beginning to brown. Serve.

Calories 334;
Fat 28g;
Carbs 8g;
Protein 14g;

Olive Garden Stuffed Mushrooms

Difficulty ●○○

Cost $ $ $

Servings 6

Preparation Time........... 10 min

Cooking Time.................. 45 min

- 12 fresh mushrooms, washed, de-stemmed, and dried
- 1 teaspoon flat leaf parsley, minced
- 1/4 teaspoon dry oregano
- 1/4 cup + 1 tablespoon butter, divided; melted, cooled
- 1/4 cup mozzarella cheese, finely grated
- Some fresh parsley for garnish
- Stuffing:
1 can (6 ounces) clams, drained, finely minced; save 1/4 cup of juice

- 1 green onion, finely minced
- 1 egg, beaten
- 1/2 teaspoon garlic, minced
- 1/8 Teaspoon garlic salt
- 1/2 cup Italian breadcrumbs
- 1 tablespoon red bell pepper, finely diced
- 2 tablespoons parmesan cheese, finely grated
- 1 tablespoon Romano cheese, finely grated
- 2 tablespoons mozzarella cheese, finely grated

1. Preheat the oven to 350 Fahrenheit and grease a small baking pan. Thoroughly mix all the stuffing ingredients EXCEPT the clam juice and the cheeses. When everything is blended, add in the clam juice and mix again. Next, add in the cheeses and continue mixing.
2. Stuff each of the mushrooms with about 1 1/2 teaspoons of the mixture. Pour 1 tablespoon of the butter into the baking pan and arrange the mushrooms on the pan.
3. Then mix 1/4 cup of the melted butter with the oregano and the parsley. Pour the butter mixture over the mushrooms.
4. Cover the pan with a lid or foil and bake for 35-40 minutes. Uncover the mushrooms and sprinkle the remaining mozzarella cheese over the top. Bake for another few minutes, until the cheese melts. Transfer to a serving plate. Garnish with parsley, if desired.

Calories 370;
Fat 29g;
Carbs 16g;
Protein 14g

P.F. Chang Spicy Green Beans

Difficulty ●○○

Cost $ $ $

Servings 4

Preparation Time........... 10 min

Cooking Time.................. 10 min

- 1-pound green beans, rinsed and trimmed
- 2 tablespoons fresh ginger, grated
- 2 tablespoons garlic, minced
- 2 tablespoons cooking oil
- 1/4 cup water

- Sauce:
- 2 tablespoons soy sauce
- 1 tablespoon rice vinegar
- 2 teaspoons sugar
- 2 tablespoons Szechuan peppercorn

1. Combine all the sauce ingredients in a bowl. Bring some water to a boil and add the green beans. Cook for 3 to 5 minutes, or until crispy.

2. Sauté the garlic and ginger in the oil. When the mixture becomes aromatic, add in the green beans and cook for 2 to 3 minutes, or until soft. Add in the sauce and continue stirring the beans. Serve.

Calories 117.4;
Fat 7.1 g;
Carbs 12.4g;
Protein 3.3 g.

Applebee Veggie Patch Pizza

Difficulty ● ○ ○

Cost $ $ $

Servings   Servings: Makes 1 10-inch pizza

Preparation Time............ 5 min

Cooking Time................... 10 min

- 1 (10-inch) flour tortilla
- 1 teaspoon olive oil
- 1/2 cup hot spinach and artichoke dip
- 1/4 cup tomatoes, diced
- 1/2 cup mushrooms, sliced
- Salt and pepper to taste

- 1/4 teaspoon garlic powder
- 1/2 teaspoon Italian seasoning
- 1/2 cup mozzarella cheese, shredded
- 1 tablespoon Parmesan/Romano cheese, shredded

1. Preheat the oven to 350°F. If you are using a pizza stone, place it in the oven to get hot. (Even though you are using a tortilla for the crust, the pizza stone will help make it crispy.)
2. With a pastry brush, brush the tortilla on both sides with olive oil. Place the tortilla on the pizza stone, and top it with the spinach and artichoke dip, diced tomatoes, and mushrooms. Sprinkle the spices on the top of the tomatoes and mushrooms, and top with the cheeses. Bake for approximately 10 minutes or until the cheese is melted and bubbly.

Calories 151;
Fat 9g;
Carbs 10.3g;
Protein 7.4g

Applebee Vegetable Medley

Difficulty ● ○ ○

Cost $ $ $

Servings 4

Preparation Time............ 15 min

Cooking Time................... 10 min

- 1/2 pound cold, fresh zucchini, sliced in half moons
- 1/2 pound cold, fresh yellow squash, sliced in half moons
- 1/4 pound cold red pepper, julienned in strips 1/4-inch thick
- 1/4 pound cold carrots, cut in 1/4-inch strips a few inches long

- 1/4 pound cold red onions, thinly sliced
- 1 cold, small corn cob, cut crosswise in 1" segments
- 3 tablespoons cold butter or margarine
- 1 teaspoon salt
- 1 teaspoon sugar
- 1/2 teaspoon granulated garlic
- 1 teaspoon Worcestershire sauce
- 1 teaspoon soy sauce
- 2 teaspoons fresh or dried parsley

1. Wash, peel, and cut your vegetables as appropriate.
2. In a saucepan, heat the butter over medium-high heat. Once it is hot, add it the salt, sugar, and garlic.
3. Add the carrots, squash, and zucchini, and when they start to soften add the rest of the vegetables and cook for a couple of minutes.
4. Add the Worcestershire sauce, soy sauce and parsley. Stir to combine and coat the vegetables.
5. When all the vegetables are cooked to your preference, serve.

Calories 170;
Fat 2g;
Carbs 18g;
Protein 15g;

PF Chang Shanghai Cucumbers

Difficulty ● ○ ○

Cost $ $ $

Servings 4

Preparation Time............ 5 min

Cooking Time................... /

- 2 English cucumbers, peeled and chopped
- 3 tablespoons soy sauce
- 1/2 teaspoon sesame oil
- 1 teaspoon white vinegar
- Sprinkle of toasted sesame seeds

1. Stir together the soy sauce, sesame oil and vinegar in a serving dish. Add the cucumbers and toss to coat. Sprinkle with the sesame seeds.

Calories 70;
Fat 3g;
Carbs 7g;
Protein 4g;

Chili Black Bean

Difficulty ●○○

Cost $ $ $

Servings 6

Preparation Time............ 5 min

Cooking Time................... 25 min

- 2 cans (15.5 ounces each) black beans
- 1/2 teaspoon sugar
- 1 teaspoon ground cumin
- 1 teaspoon chili powder
- 1/2 teaspoon garlic powder
- 2 tablespoon red onion, diced finely
- 1/2 teaspoon fresh cilantro, minced (optional)
- 1/2 cup water
- Salt and black pepper to taste
- Pico de Gallo and or sour cream for garnish (optional)

1. Combine the beans, sugar, cumin, chili powder, garlic, onion, cilantro (if using), and water in a saucepan and mix well. Over medium-low heat, let the bean mixture simmer for about 20-25 minutes. Season with salt and pepper to taste.
2. Remove the beans from heat and transfer to serving bowls. Garnish with Pico de Gallo and a dollop of sour cream, if desired.

Calories 143.8;
Fat 0.7g;
Carbs 25.9g;
Protein 9.52g

In "N" Out Animal Style Fries

Difficulty ● ○ ○

Cost $ $ $

Servings 6-8

Preparation Time............ 10 min

Cooking Time.................... 30 min

- 32 ounces frozen French fries
- 2 cups cheddar cheese, shredded
- 1 large onion, diced
- 2 tablespoons raw sugar
- 2 tablespoons olive oil
- 1/2 cups mayonnaise

- ¾ cup ketchup
- 1/4 cup sweet relish
- 1/2 teaspoons white sugar
- 1/2 teaspoons apple cider vinegar
- 1/2 teaspoon salt
- 1/2 teaspoon black pepper

1. Preheat oven to 350°F and place the oven grill in the middle position.
2. Place fries on a large baking sheet and bake in the oven according to package directions.
3. In the meantime, warm the olive oil in a large non-stick skillet over medium heat. Add the onions and sauté for about 2 minutes until fragrant and soft.
4. Add raw sugar and continue cooking until the onions caramelize. Remove from heat and set aside.
5. Add the mayonnaise, ketchup, relish, white sugar, salt, and black pepper to a bowl and mix until well combined. Set aside.
6. Once the fries are cooked, remove from heat and set the oven to broil.
7. Sprinkle with the cheddar cheese over the fries and place under the broiler until the cheese melts, about 2-3 minutes.
8. Add the cheese fries to serving bowls or plates.
9. Add some caramelized onions on top and smother with mayonnaise sauce. Serve immediately.

Calories 750;
Fat 42g;
Carbs 54g;
Protein 19g

KFC Coleslaw

Difficulty ●○○

Cost $ $ $

Servings 10

Preparation Time........... 15 min

Cooking Time.................../

- 8 cups cabbage, finely diced
- 1/4 cup carrot, finely diced
- 2 tablespoons onions, minced
- 1/3Cup granulated sugar
- 1/2 teaspoon salt

- 1/8 Teaspoon pepper
- 1/4 cup milk
- 1/2 cup mayonnaise
- 1/4 cup buttermilk
- 1/2 tablespoons white vinegar
- 1/2 tablespoons lemon juice

1. Mix the cabbage, carrot, and onions in a bowl. Place the rest of the ingredients in a blender or food processor and blend until smooth. Pour the sauce over the cabbage mixture. Place in the refrigerator for several hours before serving.

Calories 170;
Fat 12g;
Carbs 14g;
Protein 4g

Cracker Barrel Baby Carrot

Difficulty ●○○

Cost $ $ $

Servings 6

Preparation Time............ 15 min

Cooking Time................... 45 min

- 1 teaspoon bacon grease, melted
- 2 pounds fresh baby carrots
- Some water
- 1 teaspoon salt
- 1/4 cup brown sugar
- 1/4 cup butter, melted
- 1/4 cup honey

1. Heat the bacon grease in a pot. Place the carrots in the grease and sauté for 10 seconds. Cover the carrots with water and add the salt. Bring the entire mixture to a boil over medium heat, then reduce the heat to low and allow it to simmer for another 30 to 45 minutes. By this time, the carrots should be half cooked. Remove half the water from the pot and add the rest of the ingredients. Keep cooking until the carrots become tender. Transfer to a bowl and serve.

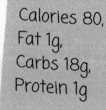

Calories 80,
Fat 1g,
Carbs 18g,
Protein 1g

Olive Garden Gnocchi with Spicy Tomato and Wine Sauce

Difficulty ●○○

Cost $ $ $

Servings 4

Preparation Time............ 10 min

Cooking Time.................... 45 min

- 2 tablespoons extra virgin olive oil
- 6 fresh garlic cloves
- 1/2 teaspoon chili flakes
- 1 cup dry white wine
- 1 cup chicken broth grated
- 2 cans (14.5 ounces each) tomatoes
- 1/4 cup fresh basil, chopped
- 1/4 cup sweet creamy butter, cut into 1-in cubes, chilled
- 1/2 cup parmesan cheese, freshly

Pasta:

- 1 pound gnocchi
- Salt, to taste
- Black pepper, freshly crushed, to taste

1. Place the olive oil, garlic, and chili flakes in a cold pan and cook over medium heat. When the garlic starts turning golden brown, add the wine and broth and bring the mixture to a simmer.
2. After about 10 minutes, the broth should be halved. When that happens, add in the tomatoes and basil and then let the sauce continue simmering for another 30 minutes.
3. Once the sauce has thickened, set it aside to cool for 3 minutes. After 3 minutes, place the sauce in a blender, and add the butter and parmesan. Purée everything together and set aside.
4. Prepare the pasta by boiling the gnocchi in a large pot. When it is cooked, strain the pasta and mix with the sauce. Transfer everything to a plate and serve.

Calories 285.8;
Fat 18.9g;
Carbs 12.1g;
Protein 8.4g;

Chipotle Sofritas

Difficulty ●○○

Cost $ $ $

Servings 4

Preparation Time............ 10 min

Cooking Time................... 25 min

Mexican Spice Mix:
1/2 teaspoon dried oregano leaves
2 teaspoons ancho chili powder, ground
1 teaspoon cumin, ground
1/2 teaspoon coriander, ground
1/2 teaspoon kosher salt
Sofritas:
1 tablespoon avocado or olive oil
1/2 medium onion, diced r garnish

-
- 2 garlic cloves, minced
- 1 teaspoon chipotle chili in adobo sauce, minced
- 1 tablespoon mild Hatch chili, diced
- 1 tablespoon Mexican Spice Mix
- 2 tablespoons tomato paste
- 1 package (16 ounces) organic extra firm tofu, drained, dried, crumbled
- 1 cup of your favorite Mexican beer
- Salt and black pepper to taste
- Tortillas and lime wedges fo

1. Place all the Mexican Spice Mix ingredients in a container or plastic bag and shake to mix. Sauté the onion and garlic in oil over medium heat for 5 minutes.
2. Mix in both the chilies and the spice mix and sauté for another minute. Pour in the tomato paste and cook for a minute.
3. Add the rest of the ingredients and cook for 5 more minutes. Taste and adjust seasoning with salt and pepper if required. Remove the mixture from heat, transfer to a bowl, and then serve with tortillas and thin lime wedges.

Calories 470,
Fat 19g,
Carbs 59g,
Protein 16g,

Melting Pot Green Goddess Dip

Difficulty

Cost $ $ $

Servings 12

Preparation Time............ 5 min

Cooking Time.................. 5 min

- 8 ounces cheese, sliced
- 1/2 cup milk
- 1/4 cup cream
- 2 tbsp. onion
- 2 tbsp. parsley
- 2 tbsp. chives

1. Microwave cheese and milk in a healthy container for 2-4 minutes, whisking after each minute, before the cream cheese Melt and mix smoothly. Stir in sour cream, cabbage, chives, and parsley. Refrigerate before serving and enjoy!

Calories 85,
Fat 7.8g,
Carbs 1.6g,
Protein 1.6g

Applebee's Onion Peels

Difficulty ● ○ ○

Cost $ $ $

Servings 12

Preparation Time........... 5 min

Cooking Time.................. 25 min

- Horseradish dipping sauce:
- 1/2 cup mayonnaise
- 1 tbsp. prepared horseradish
- 2 tsp. white vinegar
- 1 tsp. water
- 1 tsp. paprika
- 1 tsp. ketchup
- 1/4 tsp. black pepper
- 1/8 tsp. dried oregano
- 1/8 tsp. cayenne

- 1/4 tsp. garlic powder
- 1/4 tsp. onion powder
- Batter:
- 5-6 cups shortening
- 1 large onion
- 1/2 cup all-purpose flour
- 1/2 cup Progresso Plain Bread Crumbs
- 1/2 tsp. salt
- 1/2 tsp. black pepper
- 1/2 cups milk

1. Make horseradish dipping sauce, mixing ingredients with a whisk in a medium cup. Then blend the sauce until smooth, cover, and chill. Heat the shortening on a deep fryer to 350 degrees.

2. Slice the end of the stem and the end of the root off the onion, then cut through the onion, slice it in half with the onion lying on a flat side. Slice each half 4 to 5 times more to make onion wedges in a spoken fashion. Separate pieces of an onion. Mix all the dry ingredients into a medium bowl to make batter. Whisk in the milk until smooth batter then let the batter sit for 5 minutes. It should grow thicker.

3. Then again whisk the batter. Dip pieces of onion in the batter, when the oil is hot, let some of the batter drip off, and then carefully drop the piece of coated onion into the hot oil. Repeat for 1 to 2 minutes, or until light brown, frying 8 to 12 at a time. Drain onto a towel rack or notebook. Repeat until the onion is removed, stack the newer lots on top of the old lots to keep them dry. Serve fried onion slices on a plate or in a paper-coated basket with horseradish dipping sauce on the side when they are all done.

Calories 234,
Fat 14g,
Carbs 22g,
Protein 5g

Appetizers

Pei Wei Vietnamese Chicken Salad Spring Roll

Difficulty ●○○

Cost $ $ $

Servings 4-6

Preparation Time............ 10 min

Cooking Time.................... 1 min

Salad
- Rice Wrappers
- Green leaf lettuce like Boston Bibb lettuce
- Napa cabbage, shredded
- Green onions, chopped
- Mint, chopped
- Carrots cut into 1-inch matchsticks
- Peanuts
- Chicken, diced and cooked, about 6 chicken
- tenders drizzled with soy sauce, honey,
- garlic powder, and red pepper flakes
- Lime dressing
- 2 tablespoons lime juice, about 1 lime
- 1 1/2 teaspoons water
- 1 tablespoon sugar

- 1 teaspoon salt
- Dash of pepper

3 tablespoons oil

Add everything but the oil to a small container or bowl and shake or stir until the sugar and salt are dissolved. Next, add the oil and shake well.
- Peanut dipping sauce
- 2 tablespoons soy sauce
- 1 tablespoon rice wine vinegar
- 2 tablespoons brown sugar
- 1/4 cup peanut butter
- 1 teaspoon chipotle Tabasco
- 1 teaspoon honey
- 1 teaspoon sweet chili sauce
- 1 teaspoon lime vinaigrette
- Mix all the ingredients to combine thoroughly in a small bowl

1. In a large bowl, mix together all of the salad ingredients except for the rice wrappers and lettuce. Place the rice wrappers in warm water for about 1 minute to soften. Transfer the wrappers to a plate and top each with 2 pieces of lettuce.
2. Top the lettuce with the salad mixture and drizzle with the lime dressing. Fold the wrapper by tucking in the ends and then rolling. Serve with lime dressing and peanut dipping sauce.

Calories 410;
Fat 26g;
Carbs 57g;
Protein 39g

Chinese Restaurant Dry Garlic Ribs

Difficulty ●●○

Cost $ $ $

Servings 4-6

Preparation Time............ 10 min

Cooking Time................... 1 min

- **6 pounds pork ribs, silver skin removed and cut into individual ribs**
- **1/2 cups broth**
- **1/2 cups brown sugar**
- **1/4 cup soy sauce**
- **12 cloves garlic, minced**
- **1/4 cup yellow mustard**
- **1 large onion, finely chopped**
- **1/4 teaspoon salt**
- **1/2 teaspoon black pepper**

1. Preheat oven to 200°F. Season ribs with salt and pepper. Place it on a baking tray and then cover with aluminum foil.

2. Bake for 1 hour. In a mixing bowl, stir together the broth, brown sugar, soy sauce, garlic, mustard and onion. Continue stirring until the sugar is completely dissolved.

3. After an hour, remove the foil from the ribs and turn the heat up to 350°F. Carefully pour the sauce over the ribs. Cover with foil again and then return to the oven for 1 hour. Remove the foil and bake for 15 more minutes on each side.

Calories 233;
Fat 3.6g;
Carbs 6.4g;
Protein 65g

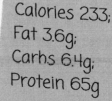

Abuelo's Restaurant Jalapeno Poppers

Difficulty ●○○

Cost $ $ $

Servings 8

Preparation Time............ 10 min

Cooking Time.................. 10 min

- 30 jalapeno peppers; sliced into half lengthwise
- 1 cup milk
- 2 packages soften cream cheese, at room temperature (8-ounces each)
- 1/8 teaspoon paprika
- 12 ounces Cheddar cheese, shredded
- 1/8 teaspoon chili powder
- 1 cup flour

- 1/8 teaspoon garlic powder
- 1 cup seasoned breadcrumbs
- 1/4 teaspoon ground black pepper
- 1 quart of oil for frying
- 1/4 teaspoon salt

1. Scrape out seeds and the pith inside of the jalapeno peppers using a spoon. Combine cheddar cheese together with cream cheese in a medium-sized bowl; give them a good stir until blended well. Fill each pepper half with the prepared cream cheese blend using a spoon.

2. Add flour into a small-sized shallow bowl. Add paprika, pepper, garlic powder, chili powder and salt. Blend into the flour until it is mixed. Pour milk into a separate medium-sized shallow bowl. Dip stuffed jalapeno into flour. Place the floured pepper on a large-sized baking sheet with a rack. Let dry for 10 minutes.

3. Pour the dried breadcrumbs into a separate bowl. Dip the floured jalapeno pepper into the milk & then into the bowl with the breadcrumbs. Place the pepper on the rack again. Preheat the oil to 350 F in advance. Dip the pepper into the milk & then into the breadcrumbs.

4. Repeat these steps until you have utilized the entire dipping peppers. Work in batches and fry peppers for a minute or two, until turn golden brown. Remove from oil & place them on a baking rack to drain.

Calories 257;
Fat 14.3g;
Carbs 18.9g;
Protein 21.5g

Applebee Baja Potato Boats

Difficulty ●○○

Cost $ $ $

Servings 4

Preparation Time............ 10 min

Cooking Time.................. 30 min

For Pico de Gallo:
- 1 1/2 teaspoon fresh cilantro, minced
- 1 tablespoon canned jalapeño slices (nacho slices), diced
- 3 tablespoons Spanish onion, chopped
- 1 chopped tomato (approximately 1/2 cup)
- A dash each of freshly-ground black pepper & salt

For the Potato Boats:
- 2 slices Canadian bacon diced (roughly 2 tablespoons)
- Canola oil non-stick cooking spray, as required

- 1/3Cup Cheddar cheese, shredded
- 3 russet potatoes, medium
- 1/3Cup Mozzarella cheese
- Salt as needed
- On the Side:
- Salsa & sour cream

1. Combine the entire Pico De Gallo ingredients together in a large bowl; mix well. When done, place in a refrigerator until ready to use.
2. Preheat your oven to 400 F in advance. Place potatoes in oven & bake until tender, for an hour. Set aside at room temperature until easy to handle.
3. When done, cut them lengthwise 2 times. This should make 3 1/2 to ¾" slices, throwing the middle slices away.
4. Increase your oven's temperature to 450 F. Take a spoon & scoop out the inside of the potato skins. Ensure that you must leave at least 1/4 of an inch of the potato inside each skin.
5. Spray the potato skin completely on all sides with the spray of nonstick canola oil. Put the skins, cut-side facing up on a large-sized cookie sheet. Sprinkle them with salt & bake in the preheated oven until the edges start to turn brown, for 12 to 15 minutes.
6. Combine both the cheeses together in a large bowl. Sprinkle approximately 1 1/2 tablespoons of the mixture on each potato skin. Then sprinkle a teaspoon of the Canadian bacon over the cheese. Top this with a large tablespoon of the Pico de Gallo and then sprinkle each skin with some more of cheese.
7. Place the skins into the oven again & bake until the cheese melts, for 2 to 4 more minutes. Remove & let them sit for a minute. Slice each one lengthwise using a sharp knife.
8. Serve hot with some salsa and sour cream on the side.

Calories 254;
Fat 24g;
Carbs 43g;
Protein 55g

Applebee Chicken Wings

Difficulty ● ○ ○

Cost $ $ $

Servings 6

Preparation Time........... 10 min

Cooking Time.................. 30 min

- 35 chicken wings
- 1 1/2 tablespoon flour
- 3 tablespoons vinegar
- 1 1/4 teaspoon cayenne pepper
- 1 tablespoon Worcestershire sauce
- 12 ounces Louisiana hot sauce
- 1/4 teaspoon garlic powder

1. Cook the chicken wings either by deep-frying or baking. Mix the entire sauce ingredients (except the flour) together over low-medium heat in a large saucepan. Cook until warm and then add in the flour; stir well until you get your desired level of thickness.

2. When thick; cover the bottom of 9x13" baking dish with the sauce. Combine the leftover sauce with the cooked wings & place them in the baking dish. Bake until warm, for 15 to 20 minutes, at 300 F. Serve with blue-cheese dressing and celery sticks. Enjoy.

Calories 189;
Fat 11g;
Carbs 35g;
Protein 46g

Desserts

Chili Molten Lava Cake

Difficulty ●●○

Cost $ $ $

Servings 4-6

Preparation Time............ 20 min

Cooking Time.................... 10 min

For the Cakes:
- 6 tablespoons unsalted butter (2 tablespoons melted, four tablespoons at room temperature)
- 1/2 cup natural cocoa powder (not Dutch process), plus more for dusting
- 1 1/3 cups all-purpose flour
- 1 teaspoon baking soda
- 1/2 teaspoon baking powder
- 1/2 teaspoon salt
- 3 tablespoons milk
- 1/4 cup vegetable oil
- 1 1/3 cups sugar
- 1 1/2 teaspoons vanilla extract
- Two large eggs, at room temperature

For the Fillings and Toppings:
- 8 ounces bittersweet chocolate, finely chopped
- 1/2 cup heavy cream

Four tablespoons unsalted butter
- 1 tablespoon light corn syrup
- Caramel sauce, for drizzling
- 1-pint vanilla ice cream

1. Oven preheats to 350 degrees F. Make the cakes: Brush four one 1/4-cup brioche molds (jumbo muffin cups or 10-ounce ramekins) with the butter melted in 2 tablespoons. Clean the cocoa powdered molds and tap the excess.
2. In a small bowl, whisk in the flour, baking soda, baking powder, and salt. Bring 3/4 cup water& the milk and over medium heat to a boil in a saucepan; set aside.
3. Use a stand mixer, combine vegetable oil, four tablespoons of room-temperature butter and sugar and beat with the paddle attachment until it's fluffy at medium-high speed, around 4 minutes, scrape the bowl down and beat as desired. Add 1/2 cup cocoa powder and vanilla; beat over medium velocity for 1 minute. Scrape the pot beneath. Add one egg and beat at medium-low speed for 1 minute, then add the remaining egg and beat for another minute.
4. Gradually beat in the flour mixture with the mixer on a low level, then the hot milk mixture. Finish combining the batter with a spatula of rubber before mixed. Divide the dough equally between the molds, each filling slightly more than three-quarters of the way.
5. Move the molds to a baking sheet and bake for 25 to 30 minutes, until the tops of the cakes feel domed, and the centers are just barely set. Move the baking sheet to a rack; allow the cakes to cool for about 30 minutes before they pull away from the molds.
6. How to setup the Cake: Make the Filling: Microwave the sugar, butter, chocolate, and corn syrup in a microwave-safe bowl at intervals of 30 seconds, stirring each time, until the chocolate starts to melt, 1 minute, 30 seconds. Let sit for three minutes and then whisk until smooth. Reheat, if possible, before use.
7. Using a paring knife tip to remove the cakes gently from the molds, then invert the cakes onto a cutting board.
8. I am using the knife to cut one 1/2-inch circle at the top of each cake, cutting nearly downwards.
9. Hollow out a spoon to the cake; save the scraps. Wrap the plastic wrap and microwave cakes until steaming, for 1 minute.
10. Drizzle the caramel plates, unwrap the cakes then put them on top. Pour three tablespoons into each cake filling.
11. Plug in a cake scrap to the door. Save any leftover scraps or discard them.
12. Top each cake, use an ice cream scoop. Spoon more chocolate sauce on top, spread thinly so that it is coated in a jar.

Zupa Caramel Rockslide Brownies

Difficulty ●○○

Cost $ $ $

Servings 5-6

Preparation Time............ 25 min

Cooking Time.................... 25 min

- 1 cup butter (2 sticks)
- 2 cups of sugar
- Four eggs
- Two teaspoons vanilla extract
- 2/3 cup unsweetened natural cocoa powder
- 1 cup all-purpose flour

- 1/2 teaspoon salt
- 1 teaspoon baking powder
- 1/2 cup semisweet chocolate chips
- 1 cup (plus more for drizzling over the top) caramel topping
- 3/4 cup chopped pecans (plus more for sprinkling on top)

1. Preheat to 350 degrees on the oven. On a medium saucepan melt butter over medium heat.
2. Clear from heat the pan and whisk in sugar. Whisk in the vanilla extract & the eggs. Mix the cocoa, baking powder, flour, salt, and in a separate dish. Drop the dry ingredients into the saucepan and combine them until they have just been added. Add chocolate chips.
3. Pour the batter into two nine by 9-inch baking pans that are evenly split, sprayed with nonstick spray and lined with parchment paper.
4. Bake for 25-28 minutes and leave to cool.
5. Use the parchment paper edges to lift the whole brownie out of one of the pans, and chop into 1/2-inch cubes.
6. Pour 1 cup of caramel over the brownies still in the saucepan, then add the chopped pecans and brownie cubes.
7. Press down to make the caramel stick to the brownie cubes. If desired, drizzle with extra caramel and sprinkle with a few more chopped pecans.
8. If needed, serve with ice cream and excess sugar, and chopped pecans.

Calories 488;
Fat 25g;
Carbs 65g;
Protein 5.5g

Applebee Maple Walnut Blondie

Difficulty ●●○

Cost $ $ $

Servings 4-5

Preparation Time............ 10 min

Cooking Time.................... 30 min

- 1/2 cup rolled oats
- 6 tablespoons butter, melted
- 3/4 cup brown sugar
- 1/2 cup maple syrup
- 1 teaspoon vanilla

- 1 large egg
- 1 generous pinch of salt
- 1 cup flour
- 1 cup chopped walnuts

1. Preheat oven to 350 ° C. Grease an 8x8-inch parchment paper pan and rows. Deposit back.
2. Place the oats carefully in a food processor and pulse to the ground. Deposit back.
3. Whisk the butter and brown sugar together in a large bowl, until finely lightened in color. Attach the sugar, egg, and vanilla and whisk until well mixed.
4. Stir in the, flour, ground oats and salt, using a spatula, until just blended. The walnuts fold. Pour batter into the prepared saucepan and spread evenly.
5. Bake until the edges are golden, and the center is set, for 30-35 minutes. (I tend to get confused on the side of under-baked blondies because I believe people prefer blondies to over-baked blondies.) Allow cooling in the pan, then use the parchment paper to lift the blondies out of the oven. Cut it into bits, and then eat. Place in a jar that is airtight for up to 4 days.

Calories 1161.9;
Fat 51.5g,
Carbs 172.1g,
Protein 7.7g,

Lion House Banana Bread Muffins with Almond Glaze

Difficulty ● ○ ○

Cost $ $ $

Servings 4-5

Preparation Time............ 10 min

Cooking Time.................. 30 min

- 1/3 cups gluten-free baking mix (such as Arrowhead Mills)
- 1 scoop vanilla protein powder (optional)
- 1/4 teaspoons baking soda
- 1 teaspoon cacao powder (optional)
- 1/2 teaspoon coarse salt
- 3 overripe bananas, mashed

- 1/2 cup turbinado Sugar
- 6 tablespoons unsalted butter, melted
- 1 1/2 egg
- ¾ cup semisweet chocolate chips
- 1/2 cup sliced almonds

1. Preheat oven up to 175 degrees C (350 degrees F). Place the liners in a muffin pan.
2. In a big bowl, combine the gluten-free flour, protein powder, baking soda, cocoa powder, and salt.
3. In the bowl of the electric mixer equipped with a paddle attachment, place the mashed bananas, turbinado sugar, melted butter, and egg; beat at medium speed until well mixed and airy. Add flour mixture, blend until the batter moist uniformly. Stir in sliced almonds and chocolate chips.
4. Scoop the batter into the muffin box, filling up every 2/3 liner of the way.
5. Bake in the preheated oven for max of 25 to 30 minutes, a toothpick inserted in a muffin's center comes out clean. Let the cupcakes cool down on the wire rack, about 10 minutes before serving.
6. Margarine cream (or butter), and sugar. Stir in the eggs and pound. Attach bananas, lemon juice, and milk. Sift and add dry ingredients. Stir in nuts (if they are used).
7. When making loaves of bread: Bake for 1 hour at 350 degrees F in a well-greased bread loaf pan. Does one loaf.
8. When making muffins: Bake for about 20-22 minutes at 350 degrees in greased muffin tins (or use baking cups).
9. Coat with a mixture of milk and powdered sugar (I never measure it; I just keep adding one or the other ingredient until I get the consistency I want) and 1/2 tsp flavoring almond. Muffins/bread glaze while still moist.

Calories 127;
Fat 4.2g;
Carbs 22.3g;
Protein 3.4g

The Cheesecake Factory Oreo Cheesecake

Difficulty ●○○

Cost $ $ $

Servings 4-5

Preparation Time........... 10 min

Cooking Time................. 30 min

- 1 (15.5 ounces) package Oreo cookies, divided
- 1/3 cup butter or margarine, melted
- 3 (8 ounce) packages PHILADELPHIA Cream Cheese, softened
- 3/4 cup sugar
- 1 cup BREAKSTONE'S or KNUDSEN Sour Cream
- 1 teaspoon vanilla

4 eggs

1. Heat oven to 350 F. Finely break 28 cookies; firmly chop any remaining cookies. Mix crushed cookies with butter; press to the bottom and 2 inches upside of a spring form pan of 9 inches.
2. Until combined, beat the cream cheese and sugar in a large bowl with a mixer. Blend in sour cream and vanilla; blend well. Add whites, one at a time, mixing only until blended at low speed after each. Stir in shredded cookies. Flow over into the crust.
3. Bake for max 55 minutes to 1 hour, or until nearly set to the core. Run a knife to loosen the cake around the rim of pan; cool before removing surface. Cool it for 4 hours.

Calories 880;
Carbs 78g;
Protein 13g;
Fat 61g

Olive Garden Lemon Cream Cake

Difficulty ● ● ○

Cost $ $ $

Servings 4-5

Preparation Time............ 10 min

Cooking Time................... 30 min

Cooking spray
- Cake:
- 1 (16.25 ounce) package white cake mix
- ¾ cup milk
- 1 tablespoon milk
- 2 eggs
- 3 1/2 tablespoons vegetable oil

Crumb Topping:
- 2 tablespoons butter, melted

- 1/2 teaspoon vanilla extract

Filling:
- 4 ounces cream cheese, softened
- 2/3 Cup confectioners' sugar, divided, plus more for dusting
- 3 tablespoons lemon juice
- 1 teaspoon grated lemon zest
- 2 cups heavy whipping cream

1. Preheat oven up to 175 degrees C (350 degrees F). Spray the cooking spray on the bottom side of a 10-inch spring form pan.

2. Measure 1 mix of cupcake; set aside to top with the crumb. In a large bowl, put the remaining cake mixture; add 3/4 cup plus one tablespoon of milk, eggs, and oil. Using an electric mixer, beat cake mixture until batter is thoroughly mixed, around 2 minutes. Pour batter into the ready-made tub.

3. Mix the butter which should be melted and vanilla extract in a bowl; whisk in 1 cupcake mixture until mixture is crumbly. Sprinkle the crumbs with the cake batter on top.

4. Bake in the preheated oven until crisp, 30 to 35 minutes, a toothpick inserted in the center of the cake comes out. Heat cake in the pan until room temperature.

5. In a bowl, mix cream cheese, 1/3 cup sugar, lemon juice, and lemon zest until smooth and creamy. Beat the cream and the remaining 1/3 cup sugar in a separate bowl using an electric mixer until stiff peaks form. Turn mixture of cream cheese into whipped cream.

6. Take the cake off the spring form plate. Use a serrated knife, cut the cake horizontally into two layers, and remove the top layer. Place the filling onto the bottom sheet of the cake; place the top cake overfilling. Cool the cake down for at least 4 hours. Until serving, sprinkle the cake with more confectioners' sugar.

Nothing Bundt Cakes
White Chocolate Raspberry

Difficulty ●●○

Cost $ $ $

Servings 5-6

Preparation Time........... 20 min

Cooking Time................. 10 min

- Chopped into small cubes, 200g butter, plus extra for greasing
- 100g white chocolate, broken into pieces
- Four large eggs
- 200g caster sugar

- 200g self-rising flour
- 175g raspberries, fresh or frozen
- For the ganache:
- 200g white chocolate, chopped
- 250ml double cream
- A little icing sugar, for dusting

1. Heat oven to fan/gas 4, 180C/160C. Grease and line the 2 x 20 cm round base with loose-bottomed cake tins. In a heat-proof mixing bowl, place the butter and chocolate, set over a pan of barely simmering water, and allow to melt gradually, stirring occasionally.

2. Once butter and chocolate have melted, remove from heat and cool for 1-2 minutes, then beat with an electric whisk in the eggs and sugar. Fold and raspberries in the starch.

3. Pour the mixture gently into the tins and bake for 20-25 minutes or until golden brown and a skewer inserted in the center is clean (Don't be fooled by their juiciness, the raspberries the leave a residue on the skewer). Pullout the cakes from the oven & allow for 10 minutes of cooling in the tins before placing on a wire rack.

4. To make the ganache, place the chocolate over a pan of barely simmering water in a heatproof bowl with 100ml of the cream on top. Remove until the chocolate has melted into the sugar, and leave a smooth, shiny ganache on you. You need to leave the ganache at room temperature to cool, then beat in the rest of the cream.

5. Sandwich them together with the chocolate ganache after the cakes have cooled. Just before serving, sprinkle them with icing sugar.

Calories 410;
Fat 40g;
Carbs 68g;
Protein 3g

Longhorn Steakhouse Chocolate Mousse Cake

Difficulty ● ● ○

Cost $ $ $

Servings 6-7

Preparation Time........... 10 min

Cooking Time.................. 25 min

- 1 (18.25 ounce) chocolate cake mix pack
- 1 (14 ounces) can sweeten condensed milk
- 2 (1 ounce) squares unsweetened chocolate, melted
- 1/2 cup of cold water
- 1 (3.9 ounces) package instant chocolate pudding mix
- 1 cup heavy cream, whipped

1. Preheat oven up to 175 degrees C (350 degrees F). Prepare and bake cake mix on two 9-inch layers according to package directions. Cool off and pan clean.
2. Mix the sweetened condensed milk and melted chocolate together in a big tub. Stir in water slowly, then pudding instantly until smooth. Chill in for 30 minutes, at least.
3. Remove from the fridge the chocolate mixture, and whisk to loosen. Fold in the whipped cream and head back to the refrigerator for at least another hour.
4. Place one of the cake layer onto a serving platter. Top the mousse with 1 1/2 cups, then cover with the remaining cake layer. Frost with remaining mousse, and cool until served. Garnish with chocolate shavings or fresh fruit.

Calories 530;
Fat 57g;
Carbs 5g;
Protein 12g

The Cheesecake Factory Pumpkin Cheesecake

Difficulty ● ● ○

Cost $ $ $

Servings 6-7

Preparation Time............ 30 min

Cooking Time.................. 40 min

- 1 (18.25 ounce) chocolate cake mix pack
- 1 (14 ounces) can sweeten condensed milk
- 2 (1 ounce) squares unsweetened chocolate, melted
- 1/2 cup of cold water
- 1 (3.9 ounces) package instant chocolate pudding mix
- 1 cup heavy cream, whipped

1. Preheat the oven up to 325 ° F (165 ° C).
2. The vanilla, cream cheese & the sugar are mixed in a big tub. Beat to smooth. Blend one at a time into shells. Remove 1 cup of batter and spread to the crust bottom; set aside.
3. Add the remaining mixture with the pumpkin, cinnamon, cloves, and nutmeg, and stir gently until well blended. Spread carefully through the crust over the batter.
4. Bake 35 to 40 minutes in the already preheated oven, or until the center is nearly set. Enable to cool, then refrigerate overnight or for 3 hours. Until serving cover with whipped topping.

Calories 1050;
Fat 78g;
Carbs 76g;
Protein 11g

Famous Dave Cornbread Muffins

Difficulty ●○○

Cost **$** $ $

Servings 6-7

Preparation Time............ 10 min

Cooking Time................... 25 min

- 1/2 cup butter softened
- 2/3Cup white sugar
- 1/4 cup honey
- Two eggs
- 1/2 teaspoon salt

- 1 1/2 cups all-purpose flour
- ¾ cup cornmeal
- 1/2 teaspoon baking powder
- 1/2 cup milk
- ¾ cup frozen corn kernels, thawed

1. Preheat oven to 400 grades F (200 grades C). Grease or 12 cups of muffins on deck.
2. Cream the butter, sugar, honey, eggs, and salt together in a big pot. Add in rice, cornmeal, and baking powder, blend well. Stir in corn and milk. Pour the yield into prepared muffin cups or spoon them.
3. Bake for 20 to 25 minutes in a preheated oven until a toothpick inserted in the center of a muffin comes out clean.

Calories 270;
Fat 37g;
Carbs 12g;
Protein 4g

Snacks

Loaded Potato Skins From TGI Friday's

Difficulty ● ○ ○

Cost $ $ $

Servings 5

Preparation Time............ 10 min

Cooking Time................... 15 min

- 1 teaspoon oil
- 6 medium-sized potatoes
- 1 cup vegetable oil
- 8 ounces Cheddar cheese, grated

- 3 strips thick cut cooked bacon, diced
- 16 ounces sour cream
- 1 ripe tomato, diced
- Fresh chives for serving, chopped finely

1. Preheat oven to 375°F. Line a large baking sheet with parchment paper.
2. Using a fork, prick potatoes in a few places. Microwave for at least 10 minutes or until soft.
3. Halve the potatoes vertically and remove the insides of the potato until there is only 1/4 inch of the potato shell left.
4. In a deep saucepan, heat oil to 365 °F. Deep-fry potato shells for 5 minutes, then transfer onto plate lined with paper towels.
5. Add cheese and diced bacon into potato shells. Place on the baking sheet prepared earlier and bake for at least 7 minutes or until cheese is fully melted.
6. Serve immediately with spoonful of sour cream on top or on the side. Sprinkle with diced tomatoes and chives.

Calories 519,
Total Fat 33 g,
Carbs 41 g,
Protein 17 g,

Cracker Barrel's Biscuits

Difficulty

Cost $ $ $

Servings 5

Preparation Time............ 10 min

Cooking Time................... 15 min

- **2 cups self-rising flour**
- **1/3 cup shortening**
- **2/3 cup buttermilk**
- **Melted butter, to brush**

1. Preheat oven to 450 °F.
2. In a bowl, mix flour and shortening until mixture is loose and crumbly.
3. Pour in buttermilk. Mix well.
4. Sprinkle flour onto a smooth surface and flatten dough on top. Cut dough into desired shapes using biscuit cutters.
5. Arrange onto a baking sheet. Place in oven and cook for 8 minutes. Apply melted butter on top using a brush.
6. Serve.

Calories 194,
Total Fat 9 g,
Carbs 24 g,
Protein 4 g,

Avocado Eggrolls from the Cheesecake Factory

Difficulty ●○○

Cost $ $ $

Servings 5

Preparation Time............ 10 min

Cooking Time................... 5 min

- **Cilantro dipping sauce:**
- **¾ cup fresh cilantro leaves, chopped**
- **1/3 cup sour cream**
- **2 tablespoons mayonnaise**
- **1 garlic clove**
- **2 tablespoons lime juice**
- **Salt and pepper, to taste**
- **Egg roll:**
- **1 cup vegetable oil**

- **3 avocados, peeled and seeded**
- **1 Roma tomato, minced**
- **1/4 cup red onion, minced**
- **2 tablespoons fresh cilantro leaves, diced**
- **2 tablespoons lime juice**
- **Salt and pepper, to taste**
- **8 egg roll wrappers**

1. Mix together the ingredients for the cilantro dipping sauce in a bowl. Set aside.
2. Preheat a large pot with oil over medium-high heat. Oil temperature should reach 350°F and there should be enough oil to cover the rolls, about 3 to 4 inches deep
3. Mash avocados in a bowl. Mix in tomato, red onion, cilantro, and lime juice. Add salt and pepper, to taste.
4. Position avocado mixture onto the middle of an egg roll wrapper. Fold wrapper on top of mixture and roll until the mixture is fully wrapped. Secure edges of the wrapper by pressing with water using your finger. Repeat for the remaining mixture and wrappers.
5. Deep-fry rolls in the pot of hot oil for at least 2 minutes or until all sides are golden brown.
6. Remove from pot with tongs and place onto a plate lined with paper towels.
7. Serve with the cilantro dipping sauce on the side.

Calories 404,
Total Fat 12 g,
Carbs 59 g,
Protein 8 g,

Copycat Bloomin' Onion and Chili Sauce from Outback

Difficulty ●○○

Cost $ $ $

Servings 5

Preparation Time............ 10 min

Cooking Time.................. 5 min

- 2 large sweet onions such as a Vidalia
- Oil for frying

Seasoned flour:
- 1 cup flour
- 2 teaspoons paprika
- 1 teaspoons garlic powder
- 1/4 teaspoon pepper
- 1/8 teaspoon cayenne

Chili sauce (yields 2 1/4 cups):
- 1 cup mayonnaise
- 1 cups sour cream
- 1/4 cup tomato chili sauce
- 1/4 teaspoon cayenne

Dipping Sauce:
- 1/2 cup mayonnaise

- 2 teaspoons ketchup
- 2 teaspoons horseradish cream
- 1/4 teaspoon paprika
- 1/4 teaspoon salt
- 1/8 teaspoon dried oregano
- 1 dash black pepper
- 1 dash cayenne

Batter:
- 1/3 cup cornstarch
- 1 1/2 cups flour
- 2 teaspoons garlic, minced
- 2 teaspoons paprika
- 1 teaspoon salt
- 1 teaspoon pepper
- 24 ounces beer

1. Preheat a large pot with oil over medium-high heat until 375 °F, not exceeding 400 °F.
2. In a large bowl, mix together the ingredients for the seasoned flour.
3. In a separate bowl, mix together the ingredients for the chili sauce.
4. For the dipping sauce, mix the ingredients together in a bowl and keep refrigerated.
5. To make the batter, combine cornstarch, flour, garlic, paprika, salt, and pepper in a bowl. Mix well.
6. Pour in beer to the bowl of dry ingredients. Blend well until smooth.
7. Chop off ¾ inches of the onion on the top. Peel, then slice until just above the bottom root end to make about 14 vertical wedges. Take out about 1 inch of petals from the inside.
8. Coat petals in flour, then shake off any excess. Dip in batter. Make sure the onion is well-coated.
9. Deep-fry for about 1 to 3 minutes, or until golden brown.
10. Transfer onto plate lined with paper towels to drain.
11. Serve with chili sauce and dipping sauce on the side.

The Spinach and Artichoke Dip from Applebee's

Difficulty ● ● ●

Cost **$** $ $

Servings 4

Preparation Time............ 10 min

Cooking Time................... 5 min

- 51 10-ounce bag spinach, diced
- 2 14-ounce cans artichoke hearts, diced
- 1 cup Parmesan-Romano cheese mix, grated
- 2 cups mozzarella cheese, grated
- 16 ounces garlic alfredo sauce
- 8 ounces cream chenese, softened

1. Combine all ingredients in a bowl. Mix well.
2. Transfer into a slow-cooker. Set on high and cook for 30 minutes.
3. Serve while hot.

Calories 228,
Total Fat 15 g,
Carbs 12 g,
Protein 13 g,

Copycat Mozzarella Sticks from TGI Fridays

Difficulty ● ● ○

Cost $ $ $

Servings 16

Preparation Time............ 10 min

Cooking Time.................... 5 min

- **2/3 cup all-purpose flour**
- **2 large eggs**
- **1/4 cup milk**
- **1 cup Japanese breadcrumbs**
- **1/2 cup Parmesan cheese, shredded**
- **1 tablespoon dried parsley**
- **1/2 teaspoon garlic salt**
- **1/2 teaspoon seasoning salt**
- **8 pieces mozzarella string cheese**
- **1 quart vegetable oil**
- **Marinara sauce**

1. Add flour to a bowl. Then, in a separate bowl, mix eggs and milk. Add breadcrumbs, Parmesan, parsley, garlic salt, and seasoning salt in a third bowl and mix well.
2. Line baking sheet with wax paper. Set aside.
3. Cut mozzarella pieces in half vertically so that you will end up with 16 mozzarella sticks. Then, for each piece, dredge first in flour, followed by egg wash, and third in breadcrumb mixture. Dredge again in egg wash and breadcrumbs for a thicker coat. Place pieces on prepared baking sheet and place in freezer for at least 1 hour or overnight.
4. To prepare mozzarella sticks preheat deep fryer to 350°F.
5. About 4 sticks at a time, deep fry for about 30 seconds or until golden brown. Using a slotted spoon, transfer to a rack or plate lined with paper towels to drain.
6. Serve warm with marinara sauce.

Calories 228,
Total Fat 15 g,
Carbs 12 g,
Protein 13 g,

Deep Fried Pickles from Texas Roadhouse

Difficulty ●●○

Cost $ $ $

Servings 4

Preparation Time............ 10 min

Cooking Time.................. 5 min

- Vegetable oil, for deep frying
- 1/4 cup flour
- 1 1/4 teaspoons Cajun seasoning, divided
- 1/4 teaspoon oregano
- 1/4 teaspoon basil
- 1/8 teaspoon cayenne pepper
- Kosher salt
- 2 cups dill pickles, drained and sliced
- 1/4 cup mayonnaise
- 1 tablespoon horseradish
- 1 tablespoon ketchup

1. Preheat about 1 1/2 inches oil to 375°F in a large pot.
2. In a separate bowl, make the coating by combining flour, 1 teaspoon Cajun seasoning, oregano, basil, cayenne pepper, and Kosher salt.
3. Dredge pickle slices in flour mixture. Lightly shake to remove any excess, then carefully lower into hot oil. Work in batches so as to not overcrowd the pot. Deep fry for about 2 minutes or until lightly brown.
4. Using a slotted spoon, transfer pickles to a plate lined with paper towels to drain.
5. While pickles drain and cool, add mayonnaise, horseradish, ketchup, and remaining Cajun seasoning in a bowl. Mix well.
6. Serve immediately with dip on the side.

Calories 228,
Total Fat 14 g,
Carbs 13 g,
Protein 13 g,

The Famous Breadsticks from Olive Garden

Difficulty ●○○

Cost $ $ $

Servings 16

Preparation Time............ 10 min

Cooking Time.................... 5 min

- 1/2 cups plus 2 tablespoons warm water
- 1 package active dry yeast
- 1/4 cups all-purpose flour, plus more for dusting
- 2 tablespoons unsalted butter, softened
- 2 tablespoons sugar

- 1 tablespoon fine salt
- 3 tablespoons unsalted butter, melted
- 1/2 teaspoon kosher salt
- 1/4 teaspoon garlic powder
- Pinch dried oregano

1. Preheat oven to 400°F. Prepare a baking tray and line it with parchment paper.
2. To prepare the dough, pour 1/4 cup warm water in a mixing bowl. Add yeast and wait 5 minutes or until bubbles form. Combine with flour, 2 tablespoons butter, sugar, salt, and 1 1/4 cups and 2 tablespoons warm water. Mix for about 5 minutes or until mixture turns into dough that is a bit sticky.
3. Remove from bowl and transfer onto a flat surface sprinkled with flour. Knead for about 3 minutes until dough is soft and smooth. Form dough into a log that is about 2 feet long. Then, cut dough equally in 1 1/2-inch long pieces, making 16 small pieces in total. For each piece, knead slightly and form into a breadstick that is about 7 inches long. Position breadsticks on prepared baking tray with 2-inch spaces in between each. Cover, then set aside for 45 minutes or until dough size has doubled.
4. Using a brush, coat breadsticks with 1 1/2 tablespoons melted butter. Season with 1/4 teaspoon salt.
5. Place in oven and bake for 15 minutes or until slightly golden.
6. As the breadsticks bake, mix remaining salt, garlic powder, and oregano in a bowl.
7. Remove breadsticks from oven and immediately coat with the rest of the melted butter. Season with herb mixture.
8. Serve warm.

Calories 228,
Total Fat 14 g,
Carbs 13 g,
Protein 13 g.

Hot n' Spicy Buffalo wings from Hooters

Difficulty ●●○

Cost $ $ $

Servings 16

Preparation Time............ 10 min

Cooking Time.................. 12 min

- 1/2 cup flour
- 1/4 teaspoon paprika
- 1/4 teaspoon cayenne pepper
- 1/4 teaspoon salt
- 10 chicken wings
- Vegetable oil, for deep frying

- 1/4 cup butter
- 1/4 cup Louisiana hot sauce
- 1 dash ground black pepper
- 1 dash garlic powder
- Blue cheese salad dressing
- Celery cut into sticks

1. In a bowl, add flour, paprika, cayenne pepper, and salt. Mix well.
2. In a separate bowl, add chicken wings. Lightly coat with flour mixture. Make sure the coating for each wing is even. Refrigerate for at least 1 hour to keep the coating attached while frying.
3. To prepare, preheat about 1 1/2-inch deep oil in deep fryer to 375°F.
4. In a separate small pot, heat butter, hot sauce, pepper, and garlic powder. Stir until butter is dissolved and ingredients are well mixed.
5. Carefully lower coated chicken wings into the hot oil. Deep fry for about 10 to 15 minutes or until wings turn partly dark brown then transfer onto a plate lined with paper towels to drain.
6. While the wings are still hot, transfer to a bowl and pour hot sauce mixture on top. Toss to coat all wings evenly.
7. Serve hot with blue cheese dressing and celery sticks.

Calories 218,
Total Fat 24 g,
Carbs 14 g,
Protein 17 g,

Southwestern Eggrolls from Chili's

Difficulty ● ○ ○

Cost $ $ $

Servings 4

Preparation Time............ 10 min

Cooking Time.................. 20 min

- 1 chicken breast, boneless and skinless
- 8 cups plus 2 tablespoons vegetable oil, divided
- 2 tablespoons red bell pepper, finely chopped
- 2 tablespoons scallion, finely chopped
- 1/3 cup frozen corn
- 1/4 cup canned black beans, rinsed and drained
- 2 tablespoons frozen spinach, thawed and drained
- 2 tablespoons pickled jalapeno peppers, chopped
- 1/2 tablespoon fresh parsley, finely chopped
- 1/2 teaspoon ground cumin
- 1/2 teaspoon chili powder
- 1/4 plus 1/8 teaspoon salt, and more to taste
- Pinch cayenne pepper
- ¾ cup jack cheese, grated

- 5 6-inch flour tortillas
- 1 egg, beaten
- 1/4 cup avocado, mashed
- 1/4 cup mayonnaise
- 1/4 cup sour cream
- 1 tablespoon buttermilk
- 1 1/2 teaspoons white vinegar
- 1/8 teaspoon dried parsley
- 1/8 teaspoon onion powder
- Pinch dried dill weed
- Pinch garlic powder
- Pinch pepper, plus more to taste
- 2 tablespoons tomato, diced
- 1 tablespoon onion, diced

1. Preheat grill to high heat.
2. Coat chicken breast with 1 tablespoon vegetable oil and season with salt and pepper. Grill for about 4 to 5 minutes on each side or until cooked through. Set aside and wait until cool. Then, chop into small cubes. Set aside.
3. Heat 1 tablespoon vegetable oil in a pan over medium-high heat. Stir fry red pepper and scallions for a few minutes, just enough for the vegetables to become soft. Add cooked chicken, corn, black beans, spinach, jalapeño peppers, parsley, cumin, chili powder, salt, and cayenne pepper. Cook for an additional 4 minutes. Stir until all the ingredients are mixed well.
4. Remove from heat and stir in cheese until melted.
5. Microwave tortillas wrapped in a damp cheese cloth for about 10-20 seconds on high.
6. For each of the five rolls, add about 1/5 chicken and vegetable mixture onto the middle part of a tortilla. Fold the edges inwards and roll tightly over the mixture. Before closing the wrap, brush egg onto the inner edge to help seal the tortilla...
7. Position rolls on a plate with the sealed edges facing down. Wrap everything in plastic wrap and place in the freezer. Freeze for at least 4 hours or overnight.
8. To prepare, preheat 8 cups oil in deep fryer to 350°F.
9. Prepare dipping sauce by mixing avocado, mayonnaise, sour cream, buttermilk, white vinegar, remaining salt, dried parsley, onion powder, dill weed, garlic powder, and pepper in a bowl. Set aside.
10. Carefully lower egg rolls in deep fryer. Cook for about 8 to 10 minutes then transfer to a plate lined with paper towels. Allow to cool for 2 minutes or until cool enough to handle.
11. Slice each roll diagonally lengthwise. Serve with dipping sauce garnished with tomato and onion.

Chipotle's Guacamole

Difficulty ●○○

Cost $ $ $

Servings 4

Preparation Time............ 10 min

Cooking Time.................. 20 min

- 1 medium jalapeño pepper, seeded and deveined, finely chopped
- 1 cup fresh red onion, finely diced
- 2 tablespoons fresh cilantro, chopped finely
- 8 ripe avocados
- 8 teaspoons freshly squeezed lime juice
- 1 teaspoon kosher salt

1. Halve avocados using a knife and remove pits and spoon flesh into a large bowl. Add jalapeño pepper, onion, and cilantro. Pour in the lime juice. Sprinkle salt on top. Mash avocado with the rest of the ingredients until everything is well blended and desired consistency is obtained.
2. Cover guacamole with plastic wrap until just before serving.

Calories 328,
Total Fat 14 g,
Carbs 23 g,
Protein 43 g,

Italian Recipes

Parmesan Chicken

Difficulty ● ● ●

Cost $ $ $

Servings 6

Preparation Time............ 15 min

Cooking Time.................. 60 min

To prepare the chicken:
- 1/2 pounds of boneless chicken breasts (about 4 breast pieces)
- 1/2 cups of panko breadcrumbs
- 1/2 tsp of garlic powder
- 1/4 cup of grated parmesan
- 1 cup of shredded mozzarella
- 2 eggs, beaten
- 1/2 cup of all-purpose flour
- Salt & pepper to taste
- Oil for frying

To prepare the marinara sauce:
- 2 tbsps. of olive oil
- 1/2 small onion, diced
- 1 can of crushed tomatoes
- 2 tbsps. of garlic paste (or 4 cloves of fresh garlic, minced)
- 1/4 cup of water
- Salt & pepper to taste
- 1 tsp of chili flakes
- 2 tbsps. of parsley for garnishing
- 1 tbsp. of grated parmesan for garnishing

1. Preheat your oven to 400ºF.
2. Take out 3 medium (preferably) sized bowls and another bowl/plate for your chicken. Fill this first bowl with the panko breadcrumbs, garlic powder, and parmesan cheese. Mix the contents together. In the second bowl, pour your beaten eggs and add 1 tbsp. of water. Mix the contents once more. Fill the third bowl with flour.
3. Thoroughly wash your chicken breasts and place them into the last bowl/plate and pat them dry with a paper towel. Season the chicken generously with salt and pepper to your taste.
4. Individually dip each piece of chicken into the flour, then into the egg mixture, and lastly dip it into the breadcrumb mix, then place it back on its tray/plate.
5. Coat the surface of a pan with oil and place over medium-high heat. Once the oil has heated, place the breaded chicken into the pan and fry for 5-7 minutes until golden brown, turning the chicken over halfway through. Place the breast pieces on a paper towel to drain the excess oil.
6. While the chicken is frying, make the marinara sauce. Place a medium pot over medium-high heat and drizzle in 2 tbsps. of oil. Pour in your diced onion and garlic and cook for 4 minutes, stirring slowly with a wooden spoon (preferably). Then add in your onions and the 1/4 cup of water, salt, pepper, and chili flakes. Stir well and allow to simmer for 10 minutes. Once the 10 minutes are up, stir once more, then add in the parsley and remove from heat.
7. Lastly, you'll need an oven dish for this step. Pour the marinara into the dish, then add in the crumbed chicken breast pieces. Sprinkle the mozzarella cheese on top of the chicken and pop the dish into the oven for 10-12 minutes.
8. If you'd like the cheese to be extra crispy, set the oven to broil and leave the dish in to broil for another 3 minutes, until the cheese is nice and golden. Make sure to keep an eye on this last step, as you don't want to burn the cheese.
9. Garnish the dish with parsley and serve warm!

Calzones

Difficulty ● ○ ○

Cost $ $ $

Servings 6

Preparation Time............ 15 min

Cooking Time.................. 50 min

- 0.75 lb. of pizza dough (either use store bought, or follow the pizza dough recipe in chapter 2 we made for Pizza Pretzels)
- 1 cup of tomato paste
- 1 cup of ricotta cheese
- 1/2 cup of sliced pepperoni

- 1 cup of shredded mozzarella
- 1/2 cup of baby spinach
- Salt to taste
- A pinch of mixed herbs
- All-purpose flour to coat the working surface
- Olive oil for brushing the pastries

1. Preheat the oven to 500ºF and lightly grease two baking sheets with cooking spray or oil.
2. Lightly flour a working space and divide the pizza dough into 4 equal quadrants. Roll out one of the dough balls into an 8" circle. Layer a spoonful of tomato paste into the center of the dough, then add a few spinach leaves, a dollop of ricotta, a few slices of pepperoni, and mozzarella. Season with a pinch of salt and a sprinkle of mixed herbs.
3. Fold the dough over (creating a semicircle), then wet the edges of the semicircle with water and gently press down on the edges with your fingers, to close the filling into the dough. Repeat this process with the other balls of dough.
4. Place the calzones onto the baking trays and brush them with olive oil. Using a knife or scissors, make 3 slits on the top of each of the calzones so that the steam can escape while it's cooking and not get too soggy.
5. Pop the calzones into the oven and bake for 20 minutes. Brush the calzones with oil at the halfway mark. Enjoy it while warm!

Calories 540
Carbs 46.4g
Fat 32.8g
Protein 14.9g

Spaghetti & Meatballs

Difficulty ●●○

Cost $ $ $

Servings 4

Preparation Time........... 15 min

Cooking Time................... 60 min

- 1 lb. of spaghetti
- 1 lb. of ground beef (or soya if you're vegetarian)
- 1/3 cup of breadcrumbs
- 1/4 cup of grated parmesan
- 1 egg
- 1 tbsp. of garlic paste

- 1/2 tsp of chili flakes
- 2 tbsps. of olive oil
- 1/2 onion, diced
- 1 can of crushed tomatoes
- 1 bay leaf
- Salt & pepper to taste
- 1/4 cup of chopped parsley
- Extra parmesan and parsley for garnishing

1. Fill a large pot ¾ full of water and a pinch of salt. Bring the water to a boil and cook the spaghetti until it has softened (about 10 minutes).
2. While the spaghetti is cooking, prepare the meatballs. Using a medium-large bowl, mix the beef with the breadcrumbs, parsley, parmesan, egg, garlic, salt, and chili flakes. Mix well and then, using your hands, form about 16 meatballs.
3. Drain the spaghetti once it's softened, using a colander.
4. Bring another medium-large pot to medium heat and drizzle a little bit of oil in it. Place the meatballs into the pot and cook for about 10 minutes, turning them regularly so that they cook evenly. Transfer the meatballs onto a plate.
5. Pour the diced onion into the pot where the meatballs were, and fry for about 5 minutes until the onions have softened. Next, add in the tomatoes and bay leaf, season with salt and pepper, then reduce the heat to a medium low. Add the meatballs back into the pot with the tomato sauce, cover the pot, and leave to simmer for 10 minutes, stirring regularly. Check for the sauce's consistency. If it's thick, it's ready. If not, leave to simmer for another 5 minutes.
6. Dish the spaghetti onto plates or a serving bowl and top with meatballs and sauce. Sprinkle parmesan on top and garnish with parsley.
7. Bon Appetit!

Calories 738
Carbs 86.7g
Fat 18.4g
Protein 55g

Primavera Skillet

Difficulty ● ● ●

Cost $ $ $

Servings 2 pizzas

Preparation Time............ 15 min

Cooking Time.................. 30 min

- 1 lb. of pizza dough (or refer to recipe for Pizza Pretzel for homemade pizza dough recipe)
- 1/2 head of broccoli, florets separated
- 1/4 red onion, sliced thinly
- 2 bell peppers, sliced lengthwise
- 1 cup of cherry tomatoes
- 1 cup of ricotta
- 1 cult of shredded mozzarella
- Salt & pepper to taste
- A pinch of rosemary
- A pinch of thyme
- 1/4 cup of crumbled Feta cheese
- Olive oil for drizzling
- Flour to coat a working space

1. Preheat the oven to 400ºF.
2. Prepare a baking sheet by drizzling the surface with olive oil. Lay the peppers, onion, broccoli, and tomatoes onto the tray and season with salt and pepper. Toss the contents on the tray and give it a good shake, to mix the vegetables with the oil and seasoning. Sprinkle some rosemary and thyme over some of the vegetables. Place the tray in the oven and let it roast for 18-20 minutes.
3. While the vegetables are roasting, prepare the pizza base. Get another oven-proof skillet/baking tray and drizzle more olive oil on the surface.
4. Lightly flour a working space and roll the dough out onto the workspace. Divide the dough into two equal parts, then using a rolling pin, roll each ball of dough into a circular shape, about 12" in diameter.
5. Place one of the pizza bases onto the baking tray/skillet and brush both of the pizza bases with olive oil.
6. Dollop a spoonful of ricotta in the center of both of the pizza bases and spread it evenly, leaving about 1" around the circumference (as this is now the crust). Then, generously sprinkle mozzarella over the bases.
7. Once the vegetables have roasted, remove them from the oven and raise the oven temperature to 500ºF.
8. Evenly spread the vegetables onto the pizzas, then season once more with salt. Finally, crumble Feta cheese over the tops.
9. You can use the second tray (which the vegetables were roasting on) to place the second pizza on, and bake both pizzas simultaneously, or you can bake them individually.
10. Pop the pizzas in the oven for about 12 minutes, until the cheese has melted and the crust is golden.

Calories 333
Carbs 26.8g
Fat 16.6g
Protein 21.5g

Antipasto Salad

Difficulty ●○○

Cost $ $ $

Servings 6

Preparation Time........... 15 min

Cooking Time................... 5 min

- For the salad:
- 2 large romaine hearts, chopped thinly
- 1/2 cup of sliced olives
- 1/2 lb. salami, sliced thinly
- 8 oz. of mozzarella balls, cut in halves
- 1 cup of quartered artichoke hearts
- 1/4 cup of mint leaves
- 1 cup of cherry tomatoes, chopped in halves

- 1 cup of chopped pepperoncini (banana peppers are a good substitute)
- For the homemade vinaigrette:
- 1/2 cup of olive oil
- 1 tsp mustard seeds
- 1/4 cup of red wine vinegar
- 1 tsp of Dijon mustard
- 1/2 tsp of oregano
- 1/2 tsp of chili flakes
- Salt & pepper to taste

1. Mix the lettuce, salami, artichokes, mozzarella, tomatoes, pepperoncini, olives, mint, and artichoke in a large salad bowl. If you have salad spoons, use this to mix the contents together; if not, toss the contents in the bowl to have them integrate with each other.
2. For the vinaigrette, take a jar or container (anything that has a lid) and combine all of the ingredients: olive oil, mustard seeds, red wine vinegar, Dijon mustard, oregano, and chili flakes, and season with salt and pepper to taste. Stir the contents gently with a spoon/stirrer and close the container.
3. When serving the salad, stir the vinaigrette prior to drizzling over the salad (as the contents may have separated).

Calories 379
Carbs 3.9g
Fat 34.6g
Protein 14.5g

Mexican Recipes

Fajita Burgers

Difficulty ●○○

Cost $ $ $

Servings 4

Preparation Time............ 15 min

Cooking Time.................. 25 min

- 1/4 C. tomatillo salsa
- 2 tsp fajita seasoning mix, divided
- 2 tbsp. avocados, chopped
- 1/4 tsp salt, divided
- 1 tbsp. fresh cilantro, chopped
- 1 tbsp. tomato paste

- 2 slices white bread
- 1 lb. ground turkey
- 1/2 C. onion, finely chopped
- 1 egg white
- 1/2 C. red bell pepper, finely chopped
- 4 whole wheat hamburger buns, toasted
- 1/2 C. green bell pepper, finely chopped

1. In a small bowl, mix together the tomatillo salsa, avocado and cilantro and keep aside.
2. In a food processor, place the bread slices and pulse till a coarse crumb forms measure 1 C
3. Grease a large nonstick skillet with the nonstick spray and heat on medium-high heat.
4. Add the onion and bell peppers and sauté for about 5 minutes.
5. Stir in 1/2 tsp of the fajita seasoning and 1/8 tsp of the salt.
6. Remove from the heat and keep aside to cool.
7. In a large bowl, add 1 C. of the breadcrumbs, onion mixture, remaining 1 1/2 tsp of the fajita seasoning, remaining 1/8 tsp of the salt, tomato paste, turkey and egg white and mix till well combined.
8. With damp hands, divide the turkey mixture into 4 (3/4-inch thick) patties.
9. Grease the same skillet with the nonstick spray and heat on medium heat.
10. Add patties and cook for about 4 minutes per side.
11. 1 Place 1 patty on bottom half of each bun and top with 1 1/2 tbsp. of the salsa mixture.
12. 1 Cover with the remaining half of the bun.

Calories 351.0
Fat 12.8g
Carbs 30.8g
Protein 29.1g

SPICY MEXICAN Quinoa

Difficulty ● ● ●

Cost $ $ $

Servings 4

Preparation Time............ 20 min

Cooking Time.................. 40 min

- 1 tbsp. olive oil
- 1 C. quinoa, rinsed
- chili peppers
- 1 small onion, chopped
- 1 envelope taco seasoning mix
- 2 cloves garlic, minced

- 2 C. low-sodium chicken broth
- 1 jalapeno pepper, seeded and chopped
- 1/4 C. chopped fresh cilantro
- 1 (10 oz.) can diced tomatoes with green

1. In a large skillet, heat the oil on medium heat and stir fry the quinoa and onion for about 5 minutes.
2. Add the garlic and jalapeño pepper and cook for about 1-2 minutes.
3. Stir in the undrained can of diced tomatoes with green chilis, taco seasoning mix and chicken broth and bring to a boil.
4. Reduce the heat to medium-low and simmer for about 15-20 minutes.
5. Stir in cilantro and serve.

Calories 244 kcal
Fat 6.1 g
Carbs 38.1g
Protein 8.1 g

South of the Border Pesto

Difficulty ●○○

Cost $ $ $

Servings 6

Preparation Time........... 20 min

Cooking Time.................. 10 min

- 1/4 C. hulled pumpkin seeds (pepitas)
- 1 serrano chili pepper, seeded
- 1 bunch cilantro

- 1/2 tsp salt
- 1/4 C. grated cotija cheese
- 6 tbsp. olive oil
- 4 cloves garlic

1. In a food processor, add the pumpkin seeds and pulse till chopped roughly.
2. Add the remaining ingredients and pulse till smooth.

Calories 176 kcal
Fat 17.8 g
Carbs 6 mg
Protein 262 mg

EL POLLO Soup

Difficulty ●○○

Cost $ $ $

Servings 6

Preparation Time............ 10 min

Cooking Time................... 65 min

- 3 cooked, boneless chicken breast halves,
- shredded
- 1/2 green bell pepper, chopped
- 1 (15 oz.) can kidney beans
- 1/2 red bell pepper, chopped

- 1 C. whole kernel corn
- 1 (4 oz.) can chopped green chili peppers
- 1 (14.5 oz.) can stewed tomatoes
- 2 (14.5 oz.) cans chicken broth
- 1/2 C. chopped onion
- 1 tbsp. ground cumin

1. In a large pan mix together all the ingredients on medium heat.
2. Simmer for about 45 minutes.

Calories 335 kcal
Fat 7.7 g
Carbs 37.7g
Protein 31.5 g

Restaurant-Style Latin Rice

Difficulty ● ○ ○

Cost $ $ $

Servings 6

Preparation Time............ 20 min

Cooking Time.................. 55 min

- 1 lb. lean ground beef
- 1/2 tsp chili powder
- 1 onion, diced
- 1/2 tsp paprika
- 1 green bell pepper, diced
- 1/2 tsp garlic powder
- 1 (14 oz.) can beef broth
- 1/2 tsp salt

- 2 C. fresh corn kernels
- 1/2 tsp ground black pepper
- 1 (10 oz.) can diced tomatoes with green
- 1 tsp minced cilantro
- chili peppers
- 1 1/2 C. uncooked white rice
- 1 (15 oz.) can tomato sauce
- 1 C. shredded Cheddar cheese
- 1/2 C. salsa

1. Heat a medium pan on medium heat and cook the beef till browned completely.
2. Drain off the grease from the pan.
3. Add the onion and green pepper and cook till the onion becomes tender.
4. Stir in the beef broth, corn, tomatoes with green chili peppers and tomato sauce, salsa, chili powder, paprika, garlic powder, salt, pepper and cilantro and bring to a boil.
5. Stir in the rice and cook, covered for about 25 minutes.
6. Top with the Cheddar cheese and cook for about 10 minutes.

Calories 510 kcal
Fat 18.3 g
Carbs 59.1g
Protein 28.3 g

CANELA Brownies

Difficulty ●○○

Cost $ $ $

Servings 30

Preparation Time............ 70 min

Cooking Time.................. 30 min

- 1/2 C. unsalted butter
- 3 C. white sugar
- 1 3/4 tsp ground Mexican cinnamon (canela)
- 6 eggs
- 1/2 tsp ground pequin chili pepper
- 1 tbsp. vanilla extract

- 3/4 tsp kosher salt
- 1/4 C. unsweetened cocoa powder
- 3/4 tsp baking powder
- 1/2 C. all-purpose flou

1. Set your oven to 350 degrees F before doing anything else and line a 15x12-inch baking dish with the parchment paper, leaving about 3 inches of paper overhanging 2 sides to use as handles.
2. In a microwave-safe bowl, add the butter and microwave on Medium for about 1 minute.
3. Add the sugar and mix till well combined.
4. Add the eggs, one at a time, and mix till well combined.
5. Stir in the vanilla extract.
6. In a bowl, sift together the flour, cocoa, cinnamon, pequin pepper, salt and baking powder.
7. Add the flour mixture into the butter mixture and mix till well combined.
8. Transfer the mixture into the prepared baking dish evenly.
9. Cook in the oven for about 20-25 minutes or till a toothpick inserted into the center comes out clean.
10. Remove from the oven and keep aside to cool in the pan.
11. Remove the parchment paper handles to remove the brownies for slicing.

Calories 206 kcal
Fat 10.8 g
Carbs 27g
Protein 2.7 g

Ground Beef Mexican Dip

Difficulty ●○○

Cost $ $ $

Servings 30

Preparation Time........... 70 min

Cooking Time.................. 30 min

- 1 lb. ground beef
- mushroom soup
- 1 (16 oz.) jar salsa
- 2 lb. processed cheese food, cubed
- 1 (10.75 oz.) can condensed cream of

1. Heat a medium pan on medium-high heat and cook the beef till browned completely.
2. Drain off the grease from the pan.
3. In a slow cooker, transfer the cooked beef with the salsa, condensed cream of mushroom soup and processed cheese food.
4. Set the slow cooker on High till cheese melts completely.
5. Now, set the slow cooker on Low and simmer till serving.

Calories 150 kcal
Fat 11.3 g
Carbs 3.9g
Protein 8.3 g

PEPPERJACK Pizza

Difficulty ●●●

Cost $ $ $

Servings 6

Preparation Time............ 20 min

Cooking Time................... 30 min

- 1/2 (16 oz.) can spicy fat-free refried beans
- 1 C. salsa, divided
- 1/4 C. crumbled tortilla chips
- 1 (12 inch) pre-baked Italian pizza crust
- 1 C. shredded pepper Jack cheese
- 2 C. shredded hearts of romaine lettuce
- 3 medium green onions, thinly sliced
- 1/4 C. ranch dressing

1. Set your oven to 450 degrees F before doing anything else and arrange a rack in the lowest portion of the oven.
2. In a bowl, mix together the beans and 1/2 C. of the salsa.
3. Arrange the crust on a cookie sheet and top with the bean mixture evenly.
4. Cook in the oven for about 10 minutes.
5. Remove from the oven and place the lettuce, green onions over the beans mixture.
6. Top with the remaining salsa.
7. Drizzle with the dressing evenly and top with the chips and cheese evenly.
8. Cook in the oven for about 2 minutes more.
9. Cut into 6 slices and serve.

Calories 373 kcal
Fat 15.3 g
Carbs 44g
Protein 17 g

Quick Midweek Mexican Macaroni

Difficulty ●○○

Cost $ $ $

Servings 8

Preparation Time........... 20 min

Cooking Time.................. 50 min

- 1 C. dry macaroni
- 1 (10 oz.) can diced tomatoes with green chili
  1 lb. ground beef
- peppers, drained
- 1 small onion, chopped
- 1 (1 lb.) loaf processed cheese, cubed
- 1 (11 oz.) can whole kernel corn, drained

1. In large pan of the boiling water, add the macaroni for about 8 minutes.
2. Drain well.
3. Meanwhile, heat a medium skillet on medium-high heat and cook the beef till browned completely.
4. Add the onion and cook till browned.
5. Drain off the grease from the skillet.
6. Reduce the heat to medium and stir in the corn, tomatoes, cheese and cooked noodles.
7. Cook, stirring gently till bubbly.

Calories 374 kcal
Fat 21.4 g
Carbs 23.5g
Protein 22.9 g

CANCUN STYLE Caviar

Difficulty ●○○

Cost $ $ $

Servings 32

Preparation Time............ 10 min

Cooking Time.................... 6 h

- 2 large tomatoes, finely chopped
- 5 green onions, chopped
- 1 (2.25 oz.) can chopped black olives
- 3 tbsp. olive oil
- 1 tsp garlic salt
- 3 1/2 tbsp. tarragon vinegar
- 1 tsp salt
- 1 (4 oz.) can chopped green chili peppers

1. In a medium bowl, mix together all the ingredients.
2. Refrigerate, covered for about 6 hours or overnight before serving.

Calories 17 kcal
Fat 1.5 g
Carbs 5 g
Protein 18 g

Puerto Vallarta Eggplant

Difficulty ●○○

Cost $ $ $

Servings 4

Preparation Time............ 10 min

Cooking Time.................. 25 min

- 1 lb. ground beef
- 1 tsp chili powder
- 1/4 C. chopped onion
- 1 eggplant, cut into 1/2-inch slices
- 1 tbsp. all-purpose flour
- salt and ground black pepper to taste
- 1 (8 oz.) can tomato sauce
- 1 C. shredded Cheddar cheese
- 1/4 C. chopped green bell pepper
- 1 tsp dried oregano

1. Heat a large skillet on medium-high heat and cook the ground beef and onion for about 5-7 minutes.
2. Drain the grease from the skillet.
3. Sprinkle the flour over the beef mixture and toss to coat.
4. Stir in the tomato sauce, green bell pepper, oregano and chili powder.
5. Sprinkle the eggplant slices with the salt and pepper and place over the beef mixture.
6. Simmer, covered for about 10-15 minutes.
7. Serve with a topping of the Cheddar cheese.

Calories 349 kcal
Fat 23.3 g
Carbs 6.8g
Protein 27.4 g

SLOW COOKER Nachos

Difficulty ●○○

Cost $ $ $

Servings 15

Preparation Time............ 20 min

Cooking Time.................... 4 h 20 mi

- 1 lb. lean ground beef
- 2 -3 cloves garlic, minced
- 1/2 C. chopped green onion
- 2 (16 oz.) packages Velveeta Mexican

- tortilla chips
- cheese, cut into cubes
- 2 (10 oz.) cans Rotel Tomatoes, drained

1. Heat a large skillet and cook the beef and garlic until it is browned completely.
2. Drain the fat from the skillet.
3. Transfer the beef mixture in a large slow cooker with the tomatoes and cheese and stir to combine.
4. Set the slow cooker on Low and cook, covered for about 3-4 hours, stirring once after 2 hours.
5. Uncover and stir in the onions.
6. Serve the beef mixture with the tortilla chips.

Calories 241.5
Fat 16.2g
Carbs 7.6g
Protein 16.1g

Licuado de Mango

Difficulty ●○○

Cost $ $ $

Servings 2

Preparation Time............ 10 min

Cooking Time................... 10 min

- 1 mango, peeled, seeded and diced
- 3 tbsps. honey
- 1 1/2 cups milk
- 1 cup ice cubes

1. Blend all the ingredients mentioned above until the required smoothness is achieved.
2. Serve

Calories 255 kcal
Carbs 52.1 g
Fat 3.9 g
Protein 6.7 g

Conclusion

Copycat recipes are the best invention in cooking since the pressure cooker. I love them because they allow me to make something delicious quite quickly and cheaply.

Copycat recipes are a great way to save money and time. You don't have to rely on special ingredients that you may not have access to or ingredients that you don't know how to use. They are also very easy and rapid to prepare.

Thanks to copycat recipes, you can learn how to make specific dishes. They also allow you to create your own personal food experience. You can try new ingredients and experiment with different flavors, and share your results with the world on social media.

Obviously, copycat recipes are great as long as you follow the recipe exactly. Don't take shortcuts. It's important to follow the recipe exactly and not change the process in any way. You have to pay attention to the flavors used, ingredients used, and ratios.

Copycat recipes are the absolute best! These recipes give you a taste of a brand without having to pay the full price. Moreover, you can use them as a great way to make money without much effort on your part.

I hope you enjoyed this book and above all it was useful. To write it it took a long time to find recipes and to test them practically. If you like, you could leave feedback on Amazon, it will help to allow other users to find this text more easily. Thanks.

Notes

Made in the USA
Las Vegas, NV
19 November 2023

80937566R10129